Look to Christ

After the signing of the Covenant between the Angl[...]
Methodist Churches, our theme for this year focuse[...]
movement of the Spirit to bind us into a closer rela[...]
within Christ's Body: 'Come, all who look to Christ[...]
(H & P 765). Read the whole hymn and notice how in[...]
is. People 'from every race' and 'from every church' are to
bring together the best of traditions of worship and prayer.
This is already beginning to happen: we read in the district
prayers of districts and dioceses, circuits and deaneries
getting together, and of new opportunities for mission and
joint ministry beginning to emerge. Let us pray that we may
learn to put aside all that divides and follow the Christ who
prayed that we might be one 'that the world might believe'
(John 17.21).

The statue of Christ the Redeemer on the cover shows Christ
far above the city of Rio de Janeiro, but you will also have
seen pictures of street people in the same city. Christians
from Brazil remind us that Christ is down there, among the
people, sharing the hardship of all who struggle for survival
on the narrow streets of the favelas. And he calls us to the
same life of solidarity – through prayer and action – with
those who are different from ourselves, whether they are of a
different faith or church tradition, a different race or culture,
or different because of the difficulties they have to bear. As
you pray, know that you are praying not only *for* but *with*
those who are mentioned, or who have written the prayers.

Cover image
Christ the Redeemer –
overlooking the city of
Rio de Janeiro, Brazil
© 1996 PhotoDisc Inc

Thank you

We thank all who have contributed a great variety of prayers
and photographs, and Norman Wallwork who, each year,
selects the prayers for the top of each left-hand page. Our
prayers and thinking are enriched by both the traditional and
contemporary. Some are commissioned and others arrive
unexpectedly. Some affirm us; others challenge us. They link
that great movement of prayer through the ages, in the
fellowship of the 'communion of saints', with the unknown
journey ahead. As we seek to follow the way of Christ, may
we, his Body, enjoy his invigorating presence, listen to his
disturbing words and make his will our own.

Maureen Edwards

Prayer Handbook Committee
Maureen Edwards
(Editor)
Susan Johnson
Michael King
Norman Wallwork
Sarah Middleton
Martin Stone

Cover design and layout
Lorna Lackenby

An outline for Morning and Evening Prayer

Open our lips, O Lord,
And we shall praise your name.
Glory to the Father, and to the Son, and to the Holy Spirit:
As it was in the beginning, is now, and shall be for ever. Amen

(From Easter to Pentecost: **Alleluia**)

Hymn *

Psalm * and *Glory to the Father*

Scripture *

Canticle from *Hymns & Psalms*

Morning		Evening	
S	825	S	826
M	833	M	828
T	824	T	831
W	832	W	829
T	831	T	830
F	829	F	644
S	830	S	832

The Lord's Prayer

Collect of the Day or of the Week

Morning Collect
Lord our God, as with all creation, we offer you the life of this new day; give us grace to love and serve you to the praise of Jesus Christ our Lord. Amen

Evening Collect
Lord our God, at the ending of this day, and in the darkness and silence of this night, cover us with healing and forgiveness, that we may take our rest in peace, through Jesus Christ our Lord. Amen

Thanksgiving

Intercession

The Grace

* See Lectionary

An outline for a Preaching Service

Welcome and Call to Worship

Hymn

Prayers:

> **Invocation or Adoration**
>
> **Confession**
>
> **Declaration of Forgiveness**
>
> **Collect of the Day**

Hymn

Old Testament Lesson

Psalm

Lesson from the Apostles (Epistle)

Hymn

Lesson from the Gospels

Sermon

Hymn

Prayers

> **Thanksgiving** (for Creation, Redemption in Christ and the life of the Church in the Spirit);
>
> **Intercession** * (for the Church and its mission; for the world and its communities; for the sick and those in need; specific petitions and remembrance of those who have died).

The Lord's Prayer

Notices

Offering and Prayer at the Offering

Hymn

Blessing and Dismissal

* Including relevant day in Prayer Handbook

Look to Christ

Prayers from which to select for personal devotion or public worship

Adoration

Come, let us look to Christ today,
for his resurrection has destroyed sin and
  death;
Come, let us look to Christ today,
for his resurrection brings all humanity
  from death to life;
Come, let us look to Christ today,
for his resurrection breathes the Holy
  Spirit on his disciples;
Come, let us look to Christ today,
for his resurrection reconciles all things
  on earth and in heaven;
Come, let us look to Christ today,
for his resurrection keeps his people
  together in unity, love and service.

Harvey Richardson,
Chair of London NE District

Thanksgiving

Let us thank God that, through Jesus
Christ, the crucified Healer and the
resurrected Reconciler, he has united us
with him and with one another, breaking
down all dividing walls.
For our unity in you and for your eternal
presence in the Church,
we thank you, God.

For the working of the Holy Spirit, which
renews the life of the Church and its
missionary purpose in Europe and in the
whole world,
we thank you, God.

For your gifts, which we have received
despite our divisions, and for having
learnt to share them with one another in
the ecumenical movement,
we thank you, God.

We pray for our Church ... may its work
be a significant contribution toward a
wider integration built on peace and
reconciliation, justice and solidarity.
Amen

Conference of European Churches
12th Assembly, 2003

Confession

Lord God, we believe that you are present
as we pray, and that the inmost secrets of
our hearts are known to you.

We are conscious of wrong purposes,
doubtful motives, selfish desires and our
need for cleansing.

Forgive and make us clean by the power
of your Holy Spirit, so that we may be fit to
serve you.

Draw us nearer to each other as we draw
near to you. Make us more sensitive to
others' needs and more able to trust you
for our own, remembering with love and
gratitude all that you have done for us.

With clean hearts and deepened
affections, may we live after the pattern of
your dear Son, Jesus Christ, who loved us
and gave himself for us. Amen

Arthur Myers, Local Preacher, Braintree

Affirmation

We belong to the Creator, in whose image
we are all made.
**In God we are breathing, in God we are
living, in God we share the life of all
creation.**

We belong to Jesus Christ, the true icon of God and of humanity.
In him God is breathing, in him God is living, through him we are reconciled.

We belong to the Holy Spirit, who gives us new life and strengthens our faith.
In the Spirit love is breathing, in the Spirit truth is living, the breath of God always moves us.

We belong to the Holy Trinity, who is one in all and Three-in-One.
In God we are all saved, in the Spirit we are all united.

© Per Harling, Sweden

Intercession

Loving God,
we bring your world:
divided by war and greed,
destroyed by natural disasters,
devastated by epidemics and disease.
We seek to offer hope for the future.
In our search for hope
we look to Christ.

We bring your Church:
broken by our mistrust of one another,
struggling to find a language
    to proclaim your word,
needing a renewed confidence
    in dealing with the issues.
We seek an awakening of faith.
In our search for faith
we look to Christ.

We come as your people
    called to live out your word:
fearful of the demands
    you make of us,
reticent to let go
    of the things of the world,
uncertain of our own abilities
    to show your love.
We seek a deeper trust
    in the love revealed on the cross.

In our search for love
we look to Christ.

We look to Christ
    who hears our prayers.
We offer them in hope,
    faith and love in his name.
Amen

Myrtle Poxon, Vice-President of the Methodist Conference 2004/5

Gracious God,
looking to Christ we see the one
who welcomes the stranger and reaches
    those cast aside;
registers a woman's needy touch and
    gives due place to each;
looks into the eyes of a child
and sees your way of trusting.

Looking to Christ we see the one
who weeps with compassion
and laughs with gladness;
tells the time to rebuke
and the time to encourage;
delights in friendship
and hints at your real presence.

Looking to Christ we see the one
who receives the gifts of others
and gives without measure;
knows when to rush on
and when to be still;
finds you in common humanity
and commonplace.

Looking to Christ this day
receive our wonder;
enlarge our vision;
and renew us in Christ-likeness.
Amen

Will Morrey, President of the Methodist Conference 2004/5

Loving Father,
as we approach your throne
    of grace,
may our compassion be increased
and the good of all people
    become our common goal.

In this time of unrest and uncertainty,
    we come to you
    for world peace;
we seek your protection
    against all acts of terrorism
    and tyranny.
We pray to you, Lord,
    for the victims of HIV/AIDS
    and famine,
asking you to enable us to be
    good stewards in using
    the world's natural resources.
We pray that the Church may be
    sensitive, bold and innovative
    in proclaiming your Kingdom.
We look to you for revival
    and church growth,
through Jesus Christ our Lord. Amen

Hendry and Rita Ponniah, WCBP
Malaysia/Newcastle upon Tyne

Lord Christ,
our local church is where ordinary people
    gather with all their needs –
    women and men,
    young and old,
    sinners and saints,
    poor and rich.
Hear us, heal us,
and bind us together, Lord.

Our local church is where your gospel is
    proclaimed
and your truths discussed,
week by week,
    in word and sacraments,
    in mid-week fellowships,
    in dialogue and debate.
We pray for all who preach
and lead us in worship,
and for ourselves in our daily witness to
    our faith.
Hear us, heal us,
and bind us together, Lord.

We come seeking refreshment
    and renewal:
some are overworked
    and others unemployed;

some are successful,
    others disappointed;
some have illness, stress,
    anxieties about others;
some are lonely, bereaved,
    doubting ...
Hear us, heal us,
and bind us together, Lord.

Here we find newness of life,
light, joy, laughter,
and all the rich variety of your gifts to us.
Help us to use your gifts more creatively,
and give us a glimpse of things eternal.
Hear us, heal us,
and bind us together, Lord.

Audrey Stanley, Local Preacher,
Christchurch and Lymington Circuit

Blessing

May God, who is the source of unity, stay
near us so that we see the pain and
divisions,
**and surprise us with the gift of
reconciliation.**

May Jesus Christ, who is praying for unity,
move us so that we feel the tears of
separation,
**and surprise us with the gift of
forgiveness.**

May the Holy Spirit, who longs for unity
with us, give us the strength to surmount
dividing walls,
**and surprise us with the gift of new life.
Amen**

Conference of European Churches
12th Assembly, 2003

Africa

Secretary: Roy Crowder

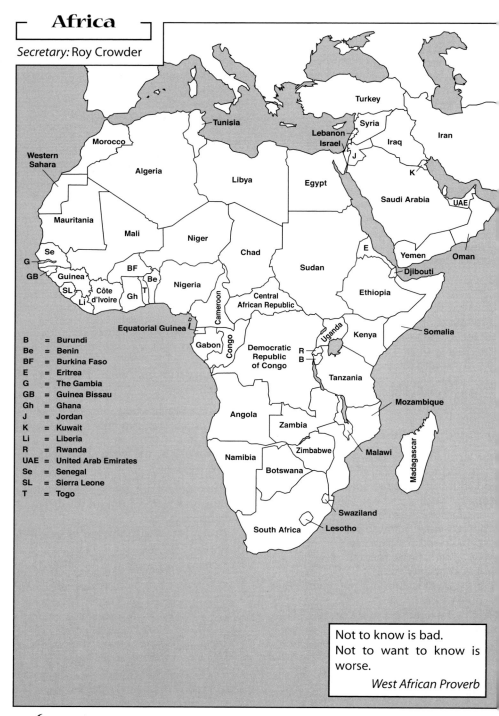

B = Burundi
Be = Benin
BF = Burkina Faso
E = Eritrea
G = The Gambia
GB = Guinea Bissau
Gh = Ghana
J = Jordan
K = Kuwait
Li = Liberia
R = Rwanda
UAE = United Arab Emirates
Se = Senegal
SL = Sierra Leone
T = Togo

Not to know is bad.
Not to want to know is worse.

West African Proverb

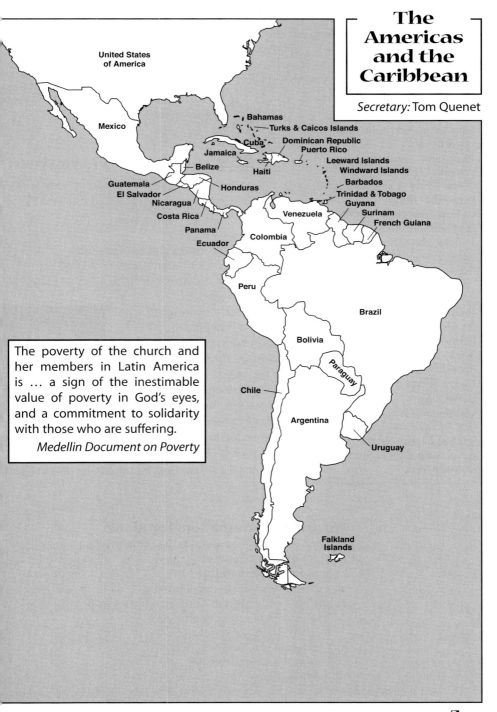

The Americas and the Caribbean

Secretary: Tom Quenet

United States of America

Mexico

Bahamas
Turks & Caicos Islands
Cuba
Dominican Republic
Jamaica
Puerto Rico
Belize
Haiti
Leeward Islands
Windward Islands
Guatemala
Honduras
Barbados
El Salvador
Nicaragua
Trinidad & Tobago
Guyana
Costa Rica
Venezuela
Surinam
Panama
French Guiana
Ecuador
Colombia

Peru

Brazil

Bolivia

Paraguay

Chile

Argentina

Uruguay

Falkland Islands

The poverty of the church and her members in Latin America is … a sign of the inestimable value of poverty in God's eyes, and a commitment to solidarity with those who are suffering.

Medellin Document on Poverty

day 1

Grant to us, O Lord, purity of heart and strength of purpose, that no passion may hinder us from knowing your will, and no weakness from doing it; that in your light we may see light clearly, and in your service find perfect freedom; through Christ our Lord. Amen

St Augustine of Hippo, 354-430

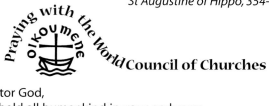

Council of Churches

Scholarship students studying in Britain:
John Ataya ° (Kenya)
Kenneth Chisenga (Zambia)
Divine Ekoko° (Cameroon)
Beni Gaba° (Togo)
Carlwin Greenaway° (MCCA)
Janet Kathure (Kenya)
John Kwofie° (Ghana)
Ava-Gail Lewis Williams (MCCA)
Titus Lunpumthang°
   (Myanmar)
Vasile Marchis° (Romania)
Joseph Michuki° (Kenya)
Ngurliana° (Myanmar)
Henry Niumeitolu° (Tonga)
Anca Popescu (Romania)
Ananda Rao° (S India)
Jolame Sedra° (Fiji)
Lawrence Shu° (Cameroon)
Layasing° de Silva (Sri Lanka)
Oral Thomas° (MCCA)
Solmon Zwana° (Zimbabwe)
Purna Sagar Nag° (Church of
   North India)

Creator God,
you hold all humankind in your embrace:
As we look to Christ, who is our Way,
may we embrace people
of all colours and cultures and backgrounds,
showing Christ's unconditional love.
As we look to Christ, who is our Truth,
may we be courageous
when faced with new insights,
generous and humble
as we share our treasures.
As we look to Christ, who is our Life,
may we be nourished
by your life flowing into us
through our neighbours –
until with all nations and tribes
and peoples and languages
we join in your eternal praise. Amen

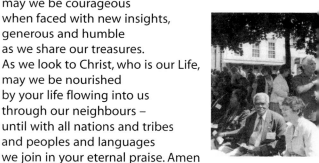

Ermal Kirby, London NE District Chair

We pray for international students

Loving Lord, may they see you welcome them,
hear your words of encouragement;
know your comfort and care
and experience your loving kindness
in brothers and sisters in Christ in another land.
   A different colour, a different race.
   A different way of speaking.
   A different way of doing things.
   A different way of thinking.
   A different way.

Jane Cullen, Scholarship Co-ordinator

Give thanks for the ways in which workers around the District, especially Deacons, 'stretch out their hands' to co-operate with planners and developers and with voluntary community organisations as they seek to build sustainable communities.

Pray for churches and projects in the boroughs of Tower Hamlets and Newham, faced with major building schemes and seeking the right ways of serving in these communities which are the most diverse in the country.

London North East District

Chair:
Ermal Kirby

Secretary:
Kathleen Burrell

Forgive our disunity

Lord our God, Creator of all life, giver of all hope,
we recognise that there are divisions between us which form
no part of your plan for us and for these we ask your pardon:

For the times when we have not worked together as well as we could:
Lord, have mercy.

For the times when we have failed to be open to your Spirit bringing us together:
Lord, have mercy.

For the times when we have not been able to recognise that unity does not mean uniformity:
Lord, have mercy.

President of British Methodist Conference:
William Morrey

Vice-President:
Myrtle Poxon

Youth President:
Christopher Cornell

Women's Network President:
Elaine Turner

General Secretary:
David Deeks

Assistant Secretary:
Ken Howcroft

European Ecumenical Encounter, Strasbourg

Ecumenical Good Friday Walk

Co-ordinating Secretaries:
Ruby Beech
Anthea Cox
David Gamble
Jonathan Kerry
Peter Sulston

Diaconal Order Warden:
Susan Jackson

For the Anglican Methodist Covenant

Father, as we walk together towards you,
keep our eyes on Jesus as he walks ahead;
and, sharing that right,
may we come closer to one another,
may we hold and support one another,
may we trust and be glad of one another;
until at last we come home to you in his strength
and his Holy Spirit. Amen

Rowan Williams, the Archbishop of Canterbury

Give thanks for the order and beauty of created things

day 2

Let my heart adore you for ever, O Lord, that waking or sleeping I may never cease to worship you. May your angels keep watch over me day and night and may the praise from my lips mingle with the songs of heaven. Amen

Gregory of Nazianzus, 329-89

Praying with Christians in West Africa (1)

The Gambia District

Chairman:
p Norman Grigg°

Mission Partners:
p   Elaine Woolley°
ad John Woolley

Give thanks that people of different faiths live together in tolerance and mutual respect and for the centrality of religion (both Islam and the Christian faith) in national life;
for close ecumenical co-operation;
for growing Methodist congregations in rural areas.
Pray for good agricultural development and good harvests;
for Church projects – agricultural, medical and educational – which seek to respond to the challenges of poverty (only half the children can afford to complete six years of education);
for a deeper commitment to mission and for a greater giving of time and money;
for the Church as it moves gradually towards autonomy.

Sierra Leone

Methodist President:
Francis Nabieu

Mission Partner:
m David Duffield

Give thanks that peace has come and that free and fair elections have taken place;
that refugees and displaced people have returned home.
Pray for the Truth and Reconciliation Commission, for the Special Court trying war criminals: that as people tell their stories they may find healing for the scars of past violence and find new energy and challenge to build a future for their children and grandchildren;
for stability as people settle back into the villages;
for the Nixon Memorial Hospital at Segbwema – an area that was devastated – as they re-equip, refurbish and reappoint staff to return;
for all who are involved in rebuilding schools, churches and manses.
We pray with ordinary people – left with few possessions – scarred, disfigured, bereaved, disabled (70,000 were killed and many more had limbs amputated)... for strength to sustain them in the difficult tasks ahead.

London North West District

Chair:
Anne Brown

Secretary:
Andrew Hollins

Mission partners:
Bernardino° and
Elizabeth Mandlate
(Mozambique)

Give thanks for growing relationships within the St Albans and Oxford Dioceses and joint meetings between Superintendent Ministers and Rural/Area Deans.

Pray for a growing understanding and working with people of different faiths, especially for the proposed multiplex style, multi-faith worship centre in the new village of Wixams, Bedfordshire.

With the emergence of a single London District, pray for a willingness to grasp the opportunities that will arise from being part of a regional District.

Dublin District

Superintendent:
Kenneth Wilson

Secretary:
Donald Rodgers

President of the Methodist Church in Ireland:
Brian Fletcher

Secretary of the Irish Conference:
Winston Graham

Secretary of MMS (Ireland):
Robert Russell

President of Methodist Women in Ireland:
Louise Wilson

Give thanks for the inter-church Alpha Courses which have led to a renewal of faith for many people.

Pray that a number of the new Local Preachers will be open to hearing God's call into full-time Christian Ministry;

that the new church in Tallaght will grow in faith and courage as it seeks to engage with the huge social challenges in the area;

for the innovative inter-church Youth Outreach being established in the town of Bray.

Lord, we thank you for the vision of inter-church evangelistic work.
May we always be more committed to the establishment of the Kingdom than to our narrow denominational needs. Amen

Ken Wilson

Look around you, look and see God's people everywhere –
opportunities, gifts and graces, riches beyond compare.
Loving God, may we never limit your love,
never narrow our horizons,
never close our eyes,
for you have so many surprises in store for those who wait upon you.

Anne Brown

Give thanks for the resources of the earth

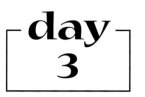

day 3

O God, whose glory the heavens are telling, the earth your power, the sea your might, and whose greatness all the hosts of heaven proclaim; to you belongs all glory, honour, majesty and praise; both now and for ever, and to the ages of ages. Amen

Liturgy of St. James, 5th century

Praying with Christians in West Africa (2)

Togo

Methodist President:
Felix Adouayom

Côte d'Ivoire

Methodist President:
Benjamin Boni

Bénin

Methodist President:
Simon Dossou

Mission Partner:
sp   Liz Rose

Give thanks for faith and hope;
that new members are being welcomed into growing rural congregations.
Pray for the Church's mission in each of these countries, in the midst of political unrest and ethnic rivalry;
that where there is corruption, the Church may uphold the values of the Kingdom and challenge the causes of poverty;
for street children who are easy victims of drug pushers;
for Assoupoe Delphine Akolly (NMA) in **Togo** who manages the HIV/AIDS project, providing education (with leaflets, T-shirts and trained volunteers) and care and counselling at its two centres in Lome and Aneho;
for the new radio station, La Voix du Protestant, run jointly with the Evangelical Presbyterian Church.

Across the barriers that divide race from race
Reconcile us, O Christ, by your cross.

Across the barriers that divide the rich from the poor,
Reconcile us, O Christ, by your cross.

Across the barriers that divide people of different faiths
Reconcile us, O Christ, by your cross.

Across the barriers that divide Christians,
Reconcile us, O Christ, by your cross.

Across the barriers that divide men and women, young and old,
Reconcile us, O Christ, by your cross.

Confront us, O Christ, with the hidden prejudices and fears which deny and betray our prayers. Enable us to see the causes of strife, remove from us all false sense of superiority. Teach us to grow in unity with all God's children. Amen

WCC 6th Assembly, Jesus Christ the Life of the World

Give thanks for new church buildings opened at Fulham Broadway and refurbishments at Lewes and Teddington;
for the expanding work of language-based congregations and their ministers;
for the sharing of ideas and concerns enabled by the Covenant between the District and the five dioceses to which it relates.
Pray for churches undergoing radical building and other changes, and for a wide, embracing vision of what their future mission and ministry might be;
for the District as boundary change discussions proceed, and for the Chairs of the London Districts at a time of uncertainty.

O Lord Jesus, because, being full of foolishness, we often sin and have to ask pardon, help us to forgive as we would be forgiven; neither mentioning old offences committed against us, nor dwelling upon them in thought, nor being influenced by them in heart; but loving our brother and sister freely, as you freely loved us. Amen

Noble Samuel, Slough

Noble Samuel is minister of two Urdu/Hindi-speaking congregations. His prayer is prompted by the experience of Christians suffering under Islamic law in India and Pakistan, and their friends and families here. Despite their feelings of anger and fear, he writes: 'They are suffering but I believe that, unless we are ready to let God help us to forgive others, we block the blessing which God wants to give us.
We think, perhaps with anger, but we need to forgive as Jesus forgave us.'

> Living God,
> inform and inspire the way we look at your world,
> that we may see strangers
>   and notice in them the potential for friendship;
> that we may see people of faith,
>   observing how we can work together;
> that we may see fellow Christians,
>   and with them reveal the marks of service;
> that we may see ourselves, with all our imperfections,
>   as loved by you;
> that, looking to Christ,
> we may see with the eyes of his love. Amen

Heather Noel-Smith

London South West District

Chair:
John Swarbrick

Secretary:
David Chapman

Mission Partners:
John° and Faith° Nyota, Cherie and Kim (Kenya)

Rose Street building scheme

Give thanks for the gift of human life

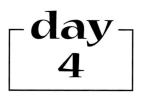

day 4

O most gracious Redeemer and King, come and dwell within us and reign where you have the right to reign. By your Holy Spirit take possession of our souls and lead us in the ways of righteousness and peace; through Christ our Lord. Amen

John of Kronstadt, 1829-1908

Praying with Christians in West Africa (3)

Equatorial Guinea

Methodist President:
Samuel Ebuka

Ghana

Methodist Presiding Bishop:
Robert Aboagye-Mensah

Mission partners:
ad/ed Ian and Diana Bosman

Experience Exchange:
Rosanna Woodruff

Give thanks for people who know how to celebrate and to make newcomers welcome.

Pray for the new partnership being developed between the Methodist Church in **Equatorial Guinea** and Cuba; that the Church in Equatorial Guinea may have the capacity to receive the gifts of those who visit, and that the sending Church may grow in its mission outreach.

Pray for the MAYC World Action Campaign linking with leaders in **Ghana** to challenge multinationals about world trade prices; for the considerable work done by the Methodist Church in Ghana in its mission schools and colleges, enabling many young people to go out and take responsibility in national and civic life; for medical work at Wenchi Hospital and in many clinics in rural areas;

for agricultural projects helping farmers to develop new crops;

for the Christian Council of Ghana as it makes local people more aware of trade issues;

that the good relationship between Church and State in Ghana may continue and that political stability may be sustained.

For all whose lives are affected by HIV/AIDS
Christ, our Saviour
'despised and rejected, a man of sorrows
and acquainted with grief',
we pray with the peoples of Africa
for hope for young people whose future is now shortened;
for children born to be orphaned;
for all who counsel and work to educate people of all ages;
for greater support from the international community ...
Lord, you made us one family: show us how to care.

Midlands and Southern District (Ireland)

Superintendent:
Paul Kingston

Secretary:
Noel Fallows

Give thanks for the tremendous growth of the congregation at Killarney. Six years ago Killarney had services during the summer months to cater for visitors. Now there is a congregation of about 70 and plans are approved to extend the premises.

Pray for the congregation at Killarney as they extend their premises to help meet the needs of a growing congregation;

for renewed vision in each congregation as the Connexion's programme is implemented;

for the work of the District Youth Council and the youth events they organise;

for opportunities and willingness to work more closely with other Christian denominations and groups.

London South East District

Chair:
Harvey Richardson

Secretary:
Russell Bates

Give thanks for growing numbers of believers in many of our inner London churches;

for signs of the Kingdom in unexpected places;

for all the Christ-centred devotion and love faithfully given throughout the District.

Pray for wisdom, among all our differences, to look on one another with grace above all things;

for an increase in understanding and compassion for all those affected by HIV and AIDS;

for creative thinking, and action, about the future of Methodism in London.

Look to Christ

How do we look at anyone?
– in the eye, from the back, in profile?
How do we get the rounded picture
of what someone is all about?
When I look at Jesus
his eyes say 'Come' and 'Belong',
but from the back, he's on the move
– disturbing, leading, encouraging,
leaving me breathless.
Every day, a loving look, then the invitation
to be moved to a new and shared experience.

Michael King, World Church Office

Give thanks for creative vision and inventive skill

day 5

Grant, O Lord, that the light of your love may never be dimmed within us. Let it shine forth from our warmed hearts to comfort others in times of peace and in seasons of adversity, and in the bright beams of your goodness and love may we come at last to the vision of your glory; through Christ our Lord. Amen

St. Columbanus, c.550-615

Praying with Christians in West Africa (4)

Cameroon

Moderator of the Presbyterian Church:
Nyansako-ni-Nku

Pray for the Church's mission in rural areas in **Cameroon** and for the continuing work of the Presbyterian Theological Seminary; for pastors covering wide rural areas with little means of transport; for Hans Njoh (NMA) seeking to improve the Church's financial management and accountability.

Nigeria

Methodist Prelate:
Sunday Mbang

Mission Partners:
p/ad   Diane Blair
d   Hans and Mary
      Van den Corput,
      Marcel and Maurice
sd/m   Peter and Sarah
      Dockree (+CA)
d/m   Julian and
      Polly Eaton (+CA)

Lord God, **we thank you** that Nigeria, diverse in many ways, was your creation; for its democracy and a peaceful transition of government in 2003 – the first time in our history. Grant wisdom to your leaders to ensure justice, peace, security and a corrupt-free society. May the influence of our biennial Methodist Conference, held in Kaduna in August 2004, contribute to reconciliation and peace in this troubled part of Nigeria.

Edoka Amuta, UCA/Nigeria

Gracious God, look mercifully upon us. Encourage Christians and Muslims to work together to help people living with HIV/AIDS, or with disabilities and those on the fringes of society. May love and understanding grow among the various ethnic groups. Strengthen the Churches to stand together and truly seek to understand our brothers and sisters of other faiths. Encourage in us the spirit of true dialogue.

M K Stephen, Secretary of Conference

Pray for Deaconess Ronke Oworu (NMA) who is co-ordinating and resourcing projects for Women's Work; for the Revd J U Ogi (NMA) working as manager of Bethesda Hospital to ensure continuity of care in a rural area; for Morin Bamgbose (NMA), now working as a personal assistant to the Prelate (presently Chair of the World Methodist Council) to ensure the smooth running of his office.

Thank God for a growing desire across the District to engage in evangelism, helped by Jan Nendick, our recently appointed Evangelism Enabler; and for mission projects in the inner city, especially 'Yeast in the City', building bridges in East Birmingham between diverse ethnic and faith communities.

Please pray for Bill Anderson in his first year as Chair of the District, John Nodding as he becomes lay Synod Secretary, Stephen Willey, new Industrial Chaplain at the NEC, working also with the churches in their Mission in the Economy; for circuits in Herefordshire as they seek to respond to changing patterns of rural life.

Birmingham District

Chair:
Bill Anderson

Secretary:
John Nodding

Mission Partners:
Florence Deenadalayan° (CSI)
Stephen° and Angela Mullings, Stephanie, Angelique and Georgianne (MCCA)
th Israel° and Leelal Selvanayagam, Arul, Ani and Sunil (CSI)

Christ of all people

On all the pathways of our lives
you are the stranger walking beside us.
With gentle persistence you press the conversation,
urging us to tell and to hear too-familiar stories in new ways.
And, in each other's telling, we catch your word
as sudden recognition.

You are the sower of possibilities.
The seeds of your fierce freedom scatter in the world,
and all the wildness of your love
springs up with yearning towards your light.

And in the bodies of women and men,
in the babel of a thousand tongues,
in the tangled threads of memories and dreams,
in the silences and songs of every people,
you are celebrated, signed and glorified:
Christ before us, Christ beside us, Christ between us.
Blessed are you in this moment and for ever.

> *Tony McClelland, Senior Methodist Tutor at Queen's College*

Lord of this new day,
   may we ask you to
     meet us in unexpected ways and uncertain places,
     blessing every congregation (especially those on the edges)
     with folk whose commitment to you
     is earthed in the strange,
     sometimes fragile realities of our time,
     and who joyfully await
      further surprises from your restless, yet healing Spirit. Amen

> *Peter Millar, a member of the Iona Community*

Give thanks for God's care for people

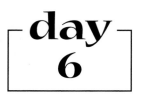

day 6

Each morning and each evening let the peace of the Father be mine. Each day and each night let the peace of the Son be mine. Each dawn and each dusk let the peace of the Spirit be mine. Let the blessing of the Three in One be mine; both now and for ever. Amen

Carmina Gadelica

Praying with Christians in Southern Africa (1)

The Methodist Church of Southern Africa

Methodist Presiding Bishop:
Ivan Abrahams

South Africa
Mission Partner:
sd Eileen McDonald

Botswana

Lesotho

Mozambique

Namibia

Swaziland

Give thanks for the Church's role in developing a new South Africa, its evangelical fervour and active concern for social issues; for hope in desperate situations.

Pray for all who work for political change throughout the countries of Southern Africa;

for all who bring relief from famine, both in aid and by encouraging sustainable farming;

for Thuthu Dlamini (NMA), Evangelism and Church Growth Co-ordinator and for her special ministry to children;

for Morgan Rabashaga (NMA) who encourages projects which focus on HIV/AIDS and the alleviation of poverty.

For the crisis of HIV/AIDS in Southern Africa

Loving and gracious God, the HIV/AIDS epidemic continues to claim the lives of your people. Parents bury their children and grandchildren every day. Young children take responsibility for their sisters and brothers. There is no one else to turn to because you alone have the words of eternal life.

We look to Christ who suffers with his people. We fix our eyes on him, the author and perfecter of our faith, who for the joy set before him endured the cross, scorning its shame, and sat down at the right hand of God. We ask it in his name.

Sipho Nyembezi, WCBP MCCA/Newcastle

Lord, we pray for the leaders of Mozambique, that they may move from beautiful speeches into actions that will enable them to deal with issues of poverty, the scourge of HIV/AIDS, malaria and cholera that are creating havoc in so many families. We pray for the victims of these diseases and for the millions affected by poverty. Help us, Lord, to provide for them. We pray for your blessings on the many faithful who always pray for us.

Bernardino Mandlate

Give thanks for new developments arising out of the Anglican-Methodist Covenant. The District is working closely with the Manchester Diocese and our Methodist partners in the Manchester and Stockport District. Rejoice with us that we are able to offer some very positive stories of joint ministry and mission. We look forward to special celebrations throughout the year and opportunities to commit ourselves further to a new engagement in mission. We look to Christ for guidance and inspiration.

Pray for the Evangelism Team and the Revd Otto Ntshanyana, our Evangelism Enabler;

for work with asylum groups in Bolton and Wigan;

for the Buckshaw development on the edge of Chorley and the ecumenical opportunities it presents;

for the Schools Forum, Property Panel and Leadership Team, as they seek to give momentum to our mission;

for opportunities in sports chaplaincy throughout the North-West;

for the Bolton Mission and the development of the town centre;

for work with young people after hosting the Youth Conference.

Bolton and Rochdale District

Chair:
Keith Garner

Lay Secretary:
Margaret Higson

Following Jesus

Lord Jesus, help us to follow your example. You noticed what others did, and listened to what others did not want to hear. For us you travelled on through so much – through the unexpected, through misunderstanding, hostility, pain, darkness and death – and on into resurrection, as you followed the vision that came through your faith. Give us whatever share we need of your loving, enduring and creative Spirit, and help us to prove that 'no work for you is vain, and no faith in you mistaken'.

Cluny Gillies, Local Preacher, Redhill

Loving Lord,
we look to Christ in seeking to serve our communities today.
Give us eyes to see the needs of people,
    lips to tell out the good news of Jesus,
    hands and feet to work for you,
    and hearts open to your Spirit,
so that, through practical love and human compassion,
we may have a vision of what pleases you
in word and deed,
through Jesus Christ our Lord. Amen

Keith Garner

Give thanks for God revealed in the prophets and the Scriptures

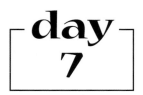

day 7

Let me love you, O Lord, my rock and my defence. My Saviour you are my one desire, my love and my helper. Let me love you in my strength and let me love you in my weakness. Let me love you at all times in all places. Let me love you upon earth and let me love you in heaven; and this I beg for Jesu's sake. Amen

Bernard of Clairvaux, 1090-1153

Praying with Christians in Southern Africa (2)

The United Church of Zambia

Synod Bishop:
Patrice Siyemeto

Mission Partners:
p   David° and Rhoda
     Nixon, Samuel and
     Christopher
ad/ad Brian and
     Georgina Payne
     (+C of S)
ag   Jane Petty (+C of S)
th   Marlene Wilkinson°

Experience Exchange:
Rebecca Pennells,
John Wall

Zimbabwe

*Methodist Presiding
     Bishop:*
Cephas Mukandi

Mission Partners:
ed   Jonathan and
     Isobel Hill, Stephen
     and Susanna
rt   Pat Ibbotson

Give thanks for the warm relationship between the United Church of **Zambia** and its partner Churches.

Pray that Evangelism and Discipleship campaigns may have an impact on people's lives and that the gospel may influence all aspects of human life;

that the challenges of the lay leaders' Conference in 2004 will make a difference to the life of our churches;

for those affected by rising unemployment.

Staff of the UCZ Mission and Evangelism Department

Give thanks for worldwide solidarity with **Zimbabwe**.

Pray with Christians in Zimbabwe for local initiatives that seek to promote peace and bring relief to those who are suffering, and for a just solution to the current crisis;

that regional governments and leaders of the Commonwealth may intensify their efforts to promote dialogue between political leaders on both sides of the political divide;

for all Church leaders and members at this very difficult time;

for freedom of speech and an end to human rights abuses;

for a just procedure of land reform;

for Zimbabwean asylum seekers who come to Britain.

In our joys and tribulations, we lift up our hearts to you from these southern lands. Forgive our national and social sins particularly when, through indifference, the poor and victimised are ignored. Awaken our spiritual vision and strengthen our will for peace, truth and justice. We pray for those with HIV/AIDS. All healing comes from you. May each one who is affected know that around and underneath them are your eternal, loving arms. Amen

Ross Olivier, South Africa

Give thanks for an encouraging year in all parts of the District: for the good response by ministers to the Re-Call Conference in February 2004. Many people have been deeply challenged in their vision for work.

Pray for the circuits as they think constructively of working together with fewer ministers in the future;

for young people growing up in a rural situation with limited employment opportunities in agriculture.

Enniskillen and Sligo District

Superintendent:
Eric Duncan
Secretary:
Philip Agnew

Give thanks for existing Anglican-Methodist co-operation, in places such as Westbury Park (Bristol); Whaddon (Gloucestershire); Bradley Stoke and Longwell Green (South Glos); Lacock and Semington (Wiltshire); Bournville, Worle and Locking Castle (North Somerset); East and West Swindon;

for newly initiated conversations across the District which may lead to more shared work and witness.

Pray for current examples of ecumenical involvement in local government strategic partnership initiatives with city, county and district councils – in Bristol, Gloucestershire, Wiltshire and Swindon;

for individuals and local congregations to develop a confidence to participate actively in the new opportunities and initiatives which can develop out of these partnerships;

for the newly formed South West Churches' Forum, relating all the Christian Churches to the South West Regional Authority, remembering Heather Pencavel (Ecumenical Advisor for Regional Affairs) and Ward Jones (Chair of the Forum).

Bristol District

Chair:
Ward Jones

Secretary:
Carrie Seaton

Mission Partners:
Ajay° and Latika Singh, Shekinah and Sharon (Church of North India)

Lord, as this day unfolds,
help me to remember that you are in company
with me.
May I flourish through what you say to me in those I meet.
Strengthen me to share what I know of you
in challenging and helpful ways.
Remind me to own and rejoice in all that is good.
Encourage me when the going is tough.
Nurture me to develop the creative gifts you have given me.
May others be touched by your blessing
through what I say and do
and, in all things, may your name be glorified.

Ward Jones

Give thanks for God's supreme revelation in Christ

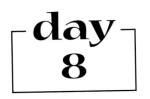

day 8

O Holy Spirit, giver of life and light, breath of all creatures, purifier of all souls and healer of all wounds, be fire to my heart, light to my path and friend for my journey; and this for your own love's sake. Amen

Hildegard of Bingen, 1098-1179

Praying with Christians in East Africa

Kenya

(Tanzania and Uganda)

Methodist Presiding Bishop:
Stephen Kanyaru M'Impwii

Mission Partners:
n   Barbara Dickinson
d   Else Iverson (+CA)
sd/d   Paul and Rachel Lindoewood, Hannah and Michael
sp/d   Paul McMaster
p   Andrew° and Sheila Moffoot, Timothy and Samuel
d   David and Mary Sarson (+CA)
d   Claire Smithson
th   Caroline° and Andrew° Wickens, Matthew and Catherine (+CMS)

An African Lament

God, our strong and steady guardian,
who keeps us in your stomach,
carries us on your back
and ties us round your arm like a bracelet ...
we rise to greet you in the morning.
As you smile upon us through the warm rays of the sun,
God of many colours, listen to us!

Our continent lies on the ground – prostrate.
Poverty, disease and war have joined hands to exterminate us.
God of many colours, will you keep quiet for ever?

You, who are the red light of dawn,
our forebears trusted you and were not disappointed.
Have you not heard, O God,
the gleeful laughter of the so-called G-8
as they spread their tentacles of globalisation,
and Africa still cries out in the grip of poverty, disease and death,
and all that others can say is: 'Give them loans', 'more loans'.
Will you keep quiet for ever, O God?

Jonathan Gichaara, Kenya,
World Church Tutor, Urban Theology Unit, Sheffield

For those with HIV/AIDS

When they are lonely, frightened, without hope,
and the world seems to crumble around them,
when they are in pain and anxious about the future,
loving God, comfort them. As your peace descends,
reveal yourself to them, so that, believing in your salvation,
they may rise above their suffering
and know the reality of eternal life. Amen

Jane Bugambi, Uganda, student at the UCA

Pray for Esther Asiimwe Betongyeza (NMA), working with women and young people in Uganda, setting up projects and clubs.

Give thanks for the initiative of churches and circuits responding to 'Our Calling', especially in areas of social deprivation and with limited resources;

for ecumenical training developments at St. Michael's Cardiff and Bangor;

for the work of NCH Cymru with children and families.

Pray for Stephen Roe and his family, appointed to serve as a Deacon on Ynys Môn (Anglesey) and for the Bangor and Holyhead and Môn ac Arfon circuits as they work out their mission in a bilingual context;

for ministry in rural areas and in the medium of Welsh;

for ministry in the villages and towns of mid Wales, and for the former urban centres in North East Wales, as they seek to respond to a time of economic change;

for the development of inter-faith work and ministry with asylum seekers in South Wales cities.

> Arglwydd Dduw,
> a ddaethost atom yng Nghrist Iesu;
> diolchwn i ti am y cyfle newydd
> yr wyt yn ei roi i'th bobl;
> yn berthynas newydd â thi ac â 'n gilydd.
> Defnyddia ni, bob un, i godi pontydd rhwng pobloedd
> ac i garu a derbyn eraill.
> Yn enw Iesu Grist. Amen

Philip Barnett
translated into English on p.78

God, our Mother and Father,
source of our being and always faithful,
you lead us with bonds of love,
and run to meet us when we are lost.
You nurture and restore us.

Enlarge our vision to cross the boundaries
of language, culture, faith and tradition.
Deepen our love and commitment to you
and to the building of your Kingdom.

Barbara Bircumshaw

South Wales
Chair:
William Morrey

Acting Chair:
Graeme Halls

Secretary:
John Williams

Cymru
Chair:
Patrick Slattery

Secretary:
Dennis Griffiths

North Wales
Chair:
Barbara Bircumshaw

Secretary:
Trevor Pratt

Mission Partners:
Edson° and Sammie
Dube, Nomthandazo
and Nozipho
(Zimbabwe)

Y Gymanfa:
Y Llywydd:
Philip Barnett

Executive Officer:
Chris Mainwaring

Treasurer:
Anthony Gregory

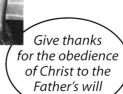

*Give thanks
for the obedience
of Christ to the
Father's will*

day 9

O consuming fire, O Spirit of love, descend into the depth of my heart and there transform me until I am fire of your fire, love of your love, and Christ himself is formed in me. Amen

Elizabeth of Schonau, d.1184

Praying with Christians **in South America (1)**

Brazil

Methodist Bishop:
João Alves de Oliveira Filho

Uruguay

Methodist President:
Oscar Bolioli

Argentina

Methodist Bishop:
Nelly Ritchie

Mission Partner:
p   Sue Jansen°

Colombia

Methodist Bishop:
Isaías Gutiérrez

Ecuador

Methodist Bishop:
Salomón Cabezas

Pray for Nationals in Mission (NMAs):
Cleonice de Quieroz Henrique Nery, working with women and young people in **Brazil** to explore ways to trade their goods for a fair price in the world market;
Maria Moreira Lima, providing care and rehabilitation for impoverished young people and their families in Brazil;
Jose Carlos do Prado Ramos, co-ordinating a project for street people in Sao Paulo, Brazil;
Anibal Siccardi, Secretary for Publications and Communications, co-ordinating a wide range of activities in **Uruguay**;
David Ludena Idrovo, organising health care and education programmes and developing faith and discipleship in **Ecuador**;
Eduardo Morales Vega, developing pastoral care, social outreach and evangelism in Ecuador;
Gabriela Amaya de Fernandez, developing Christian educational materials and training teachers in **Argentina**;

CLAI, the Latin American Council of Churches calls on all Churches worldwide to practical solidarity with those in greatest need. Poverty in Latin America is aggravated by multinational companies who pillage its natural resources and exploit its people's labour. The world is called to repentance and changed lives, so that all may enjoy what God has provided.

Lord, have mercy.
Forgive us that the food we eat, and the commodities we enjoy
    come at the expense of the world's poor.
Increase within us the will to put the values of your Kingdom
    before profit and the acquisition of property and possessions,
that we may stand with those who are victims of the free market.
Through our action,
    may all people live with joy, in peace and harmony.
How beautiful is life when we seek truth, justice and freedom ...

Based on a Pastoral Letter, Buenos Aires

Give thanks for Churches Together in Cumbria, for the churches of Cumbria working in partnership with each other and with secular agencies in urban and rural regeneration projects.

Pray for Community Action Furness, a project in Barrow initiated by the churches and helping to create employment opportunities in the Furness area;

for Hidden Britain Centres, a project of the Arthur Rank Centre, offering new opportunities for visitors to enjoy the landscape and culture of Cumbria;

for growing relationships in Anglican Deaneries and Methodist Circuits and a new partnership between the United Reformed Church in Cumbria and the Methodist District.

Cumbria District

Chair:
David Emison

Secretary:
David Andrews

For peace

I had a box of coloured paints
but it did not contain red
for the blood of the wounded
nor white
for the hands and faces of the dead,
neither did it contain yellow
for the burning sands of the desert.
Instead it had orange for dawn and dusk,
and sky blue for the new skies,
and pink for young dreams,
I sat and painted peace.

Prayer by a 10-year old boy from Brazil

The mist enfolds the hills in its mantle:
    Embrace us in your love, O Lord.
The rain washes the rocks and leaves:
    Cleanse us in your love, O Lord.
The beck tumbles down to the valley:
    Direct us in your love, O Lord.
The mountain peaks stand firm:
    Establish us in your love, O Lord.
The rowan tree clings to the side of the gill:
    Root us in your love, O Lord.
The night veils the fells in darkness:
    Hide us in your love, O Lord.

John Biggs, Ambleside

Give thanks for the value Christ gave to human labour

25

day 10

Knit my soul to your own, O Christ, so that I may never be separated from you. Only in you am I a person fully alive. Only in your light can I see and only in your strength can I pursue my way. To you I come, O wisdom without end. In you I rest, O mercy without limit. To you I give all praise, O crown of all majesty.

Mechtild of Magdeburg, 1210-1280

Praying with Christians in South America (2)

Bolivia

Methodist Bishop:
Carlos Intipampa

Chile

Methodist Bishop:
Pedro Grandon

Mission Partner:
p Thomasina Elers

Peru

Methodist Bishop:
Marco Ochoa

rt   Margaret° and
Aldo Valle

Give thanks for people of faith in each of these countries who are sustained in the struggle;
for Casimira Rodriguez Romero, a campaigner for the rights of domestic workers in **Bolivia**, who has won the Methodist Peace Award: 'a gentle Christian' whose faith and commitment have sustained her in the face of overwhelming adversity;
for growing churches in **Chile**, vibrant worship, and for strength of faith in the midst of economic difficulties;
for groups of young people at school and university meeting to study the Bible and develop their faith.

Pray for the training of lay leaders and for the building up of the life of local congregations in **Bolivia**;
for the deepening of faith and strength to combat social evils;
for all ministers and church leaders working out their mission in the context of poverty and social unrest;
for a stable government and a fair distribution of resources.

Pray for women who suffer abuse and discrimination in **Chile** and for children of single mothers who do not have ready access to education;
for the ministry of the Mapuche Methodist women;
for rural communities seeking to increase their stock, dig more wells, and develop organic farming;
that the Church's dream of meeting the needs of more people may come true.

Pray for all engaging in mission and social outreach in **Peru**;
for young ministers who have difficulty in responding to the challenge to serve in rural areas for linguistic and cultural reasons;
for new congregations and evangelistic work in the Cusco area.

Give thanks for the opening of the new Clooney Family Centre in the Waterside area of Londonderry.
Pray for opportunities to develop university chaplaincy ministry in both Coleraine and Londonderry;
for work among prisoners in Magilligan prison.

North West District (Ireland)

Superintendent:
Harold Agnew

Secretary:
Alan Macaulay

During a time of change for the Islands, and the search for a way forward, **we give thanks** for the continuing commitment of the people of God – in the Church and the world.
In responding to the invitation to 'Look to Christ', **we pray** for those involved in chaplaincy work to the prisons, hospitals, schools, colleges and the tourist industry within the Islands;
for the developing of ecumenical links, for the faith communities and the wider community.

Channel Islands District

Chair:
David Coote

Secretary:
Stephen Robinson

Lord of all people,
empower us to respond to your challenge
to open our minds to you,
widen our love for others
and hold out the gift of dignity and justice for all.

May your love uphold us,
your Spirit guide us
and your peace enfold us
in our commitment to you and your Kingdom. Amen

Ian White

Lord God, gracious and merciful,
you anointed your beloved Son with the Holy Spirit
at his baptism in the Jordan,
and you consecrated him prophet, priest and king:
pour out your Spirit on us again
that we may be faithful to our baptismal calling,
ardently desire the communion of Christ's body and blood,
and serve the poor of your people and all who need your love,
through Jesus Christ, your Son, our Lord,
who lives and reigns with you in the unity of the Holy Spirit,
ever one God, world without end. Amen

From the Lima Liturgy, Peru 1982
© World Council of Churches

Give thanks for the strength Christ gives to his disciples

27

day 11

Pour upon us, O Holy Spirit, your sevenfold gifts: of understanding that we may be enlightened; of counsel that we may follow in your footsteps; of courage that we may face the enemy; of knowledge that we may discern the good; of piety that we may be compassionate; of fear that we may draw back from evil, and of wisdom that we may taste the sweetness of your love. Amen

St. Bonaventure, 1217-1274

 Praying with Christians in Central America

---

Belize and Honduras District
of the MCCA

District President:
David Goff

Panama and Costa Rica District
of the MCCA

District President:
Mario Nicolas

Guyana District

District President:
Barrington Litchmore

Guatemala

Methodist President:
Juan Pablo Ajanel

Mexico

Methodist Bishop:
Raul Rosas González

Give thanks for faith and hope in each of these Districts.
Pray for children living on the streets;
for families who have barely enough to survive;
for the Church's ministry in the context of poverty, drug abuse, drug trafficking, crime, prostitution ...
for vocational courses for women and young people;
for justice and all who strive for it in Central America.

Dear Lord, **we thank you** for your continued love, mercy and compassion, and for the blessings of the John and Charles Wesley Centre in **Belize** City.
We pray that many lives will be touched by its varied activities; and that your people may have a clear vision for mission and outreach that will bring them closer to our risen and living Lord.

Stephen Mullings, Belize/WCBP Evesham

Pray for Deacon Hope McNeil Williams (NMA), working with schools, young people and parents in **Belize**;
for Pedro Arauz Valdes (NMA) training leaders and promoting the concept of a Christian family in the Chiriqui province of **Panama**;
for Margaret Johnson (NMA) , Christian Education Director in Panama, helping church and community to find wholeness through worship, prayer and action;
for Communidad Teologica de **Honduras**, an ecumenical group of pastors who meet monthly to share experiences, to support and learn from one another.

Risen Saviour, be among us as we carry the seed,
as we labour together, guide our sowing,
that the fruits of what we do may produce a harvest of joy. Amen

Based on the Mayan practice of communal seed sowing
From Encounter, USPG

We give thanks for the closer working together of Chester Cathedral and Wesley Methodist Church in Chester, involving a regular exchange of preachers and Methodist celebration of Holy Communion in the Cathedral. Together with other churches we mark 20 years of shared service in the city centre at the St Peter's Ecumenical Centre which attracts many tourists.

We pray for the Forum of Faiths in Stoke-on-Trent and North Staffordshire building trust and friendship between Christians, Jews, Muslims, Hindus and other world faiths and being available as a consultative body for the city partnership scheme and for regional government;

for the newly appointed Community Chaplain in North Staffordshire, an ecumenical enterprise funded by church and secular charities to befriend and help those newly discharged from prison.

Chester and Stoke on Trent District

Chair:
John Walker

Secretary:
David Scott

Mission partners:
Jimione° and Miriama Kaci, and Salanieta (Fiji)

World Church in Britain Partnership

Like Abraham of old, you called us to travel
  – twenty-six hours by air –
to be with a congregation that was new to us.
We had enjoyed a warm climate,
  but thank you now for the coolness of winter.
We were with relatives and old friends,
  but thank you for a new family and new friends.
Lord, you have taken away our loneliness and longing for home
by your daily presence in our lives.
Thank you for bringing us to see the diversity of life. Amen

Jimione and Miriama Kaci, WCBP Fiji / Sandbach

Inclusive God,

  we offer ourselves to enrich and enjoy the great fellowship of belonging in this corner of the universe. Like Francis of Assisi may we feel ourselves related to sun, moon, wind, water, earth and humankind as sisters and brothers because we belong to you, the Creator.

  We engage ourselves to recognise and express love as the final meaning and arbiter of all things. Like Julian of Norwich may we see love as your meaning and perceive that 'all manner of things shall be well'.

  We give ourselves to lighten the loneliness of those around us. Like John Wesley we believe that all are wanted and valued in Christ and that the best of all is that you are with us.

John Walker

Give thanks for the call to follow Christ

day 12

Be to us, O Lord, the affection of our hearts, the closest of our companions, our everlasting love, our enduring happiness and the fulfilment of all our desires. Through your Spirit, create in us holy fire and purity of life, that loving you above all things and our neighbours ardently, we may come at last to the glories of your everlasting kingdom; through Christ our Lord. Amen

Thomas à Kempis (1380-1471)

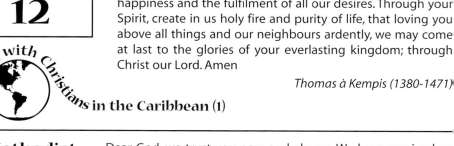

Praying with Christians in the Caribbean (1)

Methodist Church in the Caribbean and the Americas
(MCCA)

Connexional President:
George Mulrain

Leeward Islands District

District President:
Selwyn Vanterpool

South Caribbean District

District President:
Victor Job

Mission Partners:
p   Elaine° and Ewart Joseph

Dear God, we trust you now and always. We have received so many good experiences from you, that we will not complain when situations are not in our favour. We will endure strong winds, hurricanes, heavy rains, floods, earthquakes, volcanoes, and still offer praises to your name.

We rejoice, knowing you are in control. When people take matters into their own hands, with disastrous results, we will trust you. If there are political upheavals, and creative solutions seem far off, we will not doubt that you are near. Even if we walk through the valley of the shadow of death, we will not fear.

You gave to us good news in Jesus Christ. We will endeavour to live out this gospel seeking justice, peace, love and harmonious relationships among those we encounter daily.

God of us all, thank you for nurturing in us the faith that we have. We pledge to pass on this faith to our children and hope that they in turn will do the same with their offspring. May the world ultimately and visibly come under your sovereign rule. God, we will trust you now and always. Amen

George Mulrain, Connexional President, MCCA

Pray for Paul Douglas-Walfall and Marlene Britton-Walfall (NMAs – **South Caribbean**), co-ordinating training courses in Bible study, evangelism and church growth, and in preparing new material for use with children;
for Stephane Brooks and Claudine Glasgow-Brooks (NMAs – **Leeward Islands**), encouraging church growth in the Guadeloupe/Martinique Mission;
for Trudy de Verteuil (NMA – **Caribbean Conference of Churches**), co-ordinating awareness building and counselling workshops on HIV/AIDS and drug abuse;
for the people of Montserrat still rebuilding their lives with faith and good humour, and for its older people still coping with a degree of trauma, grief and loss.

Give thanks for the opportunities provided by the fact that the District, the Truro Diocese and the County Council cover almost the same geographical area;

for increasing links between District and Diocese and the development of the new Methodist District Office in Diocesan House.

Pray for Steve Emery-Wright, our new Youth Enabler, in his work with emerging youth congregations and the newly formed Youth Synod;

for Carol Mote, our new Training and Development Officer.

Loving God,

as we celebrate the signing of a Covenant between the Anglican and Methodist Churches, we are challenged by the diversity within our Christian family. We pray for the Church family of all traditions, with all our differences, that by valuing each other we may work together to develop the life of your Church. In our love for you and for each other, may we be empowered by the Holy Spirit, so that together we may proclaim your love to those whom we meet, wherever they may be. Amen

Margaret Barnes, Ecumenical Officer, Cornwall District

Cornwall District

Chair:
Christopher Blake

Secretary:
Celia Phillips

Enlarge our vision

Dear God, we know that you encourage us
when we are feeling self-centred, lethargic and unwilling to move
even a little, to be with you and your people,
our people, poor and rich, all over our world.

Dear God, we know that you encourage us
when we are too busy to move in a new direction.
Help us to see that our work or way of life may be a block.
Give us openness to look and listen, to be ready to move,
     ready for service.

Dear God, open our minds and hearts,
so that we may know something of you.
Forgive us when our visions are too small
and when we are too lazy to step outside them.
Forgive us when we reduce you, dear God,
to our own understanding and control.
Help us to be grateful that there will always be more.

Barbara Butler, Christians Aware

Give thanks for opportunities of work and leisure

day 13

Blessed Lord God, be to me at all times my unending joy, my eternal bliss and my enduring comfort. Be to me light in the darkness, strength in temptation and refreshment in the desert. Grant that, penitent for my sins, I may never be separated from you and, longing for your face, I may behold you in heaven; for your own name's sake. Amen

Margery Kempe, c.1373-c.1433

Praying with Christians in the Caribbean (2)

Jamaica District

District President:
Byron Chambers

Mission Partners:
t Paul and Mary Thomas, Christopher, Matthew and David

Bahamas and Turks and Caicos Islands District

District President:
Raymond Neilly

Mission Partners:
p Eddie° and Susan Sykes, Jonathan and Thomas

Haiti District

District President:
Raphael Dessieu

Cuba

Methodist Bishop:
Ricardo Pereira Díaz

Give thanks for all that has been received and learnt from the faithfulness of Caribbean Christians.

Pray with local churches who are addressing the needs of people in poverty around them, and for the Church's work in schools, health centres and clinics in all circuits;

for Operation Peace in Kingston, **Jamaica**, helping disadvantaged people through vocational training and medical clinics;

for Helen Mallalieu (NMA), through prayer and counselling, helping Jamaican children to rebuild their lives after a bad start. Pray for NMAs in **Cuba**: Cesar Blanc Castellanos, training local church and District leaders and Moises Isla Duenas, a specialist in evangelism, who is contributing to the phenomenal growth of the Cuban Church.

Pray with the people of **Haiti**, weary after so many changes of government and the effects of the flood, that a time of lasting peace with justice may come soon;

for the Church as it ministers in this context, and for political goodwill among richer nations to support Haiti and revive its agriculture and economic base;

for Jean Josue Seguere (NMA), working with local church treasurers to organise their accounts.

Dear God,
forgive us for allowing differences
in culture, religion, age and gender
to create tensions in our minds, our communities,
and throughout the world.
Help us to recognise these tensions within us
so that we can deal with them and help to build peace.
Enable us to hear and answer your call to be one people,
so that all the world may believe in you. Amen

Constance Magnus, Jamaica

Give thanks for the work at the Church of the Good Shepherd. This is a shared Church with the Church of Ireland and it is working well under the new Covenant Scheme. Its minister is Alan Lorimer. Give thanks for the increase in numbers involved in our youth and children's work, and for the desire of many of our churches to reach out in practical ways into local communities.

Please pray for our new District Superintendent, Aian Ferguson; for the work of our chaplains in the University of Ulster at Jordanstown and in the area and local hospitals; for the social outreach of our Newtownabbey Mission.

North East District (Ireland)

Superintendent:
Aian Ferguson

Secretary:
Trevor Jamieson

Give thanks for those circuits which have been able to employ workers with children and young people: Darlington, Stokesley, Crook and Willington, Barnard Castle and Teesdale, and that other circuits are finding new ways of enabling younger people to worship and serve Christ;

for the life of the people at Carrville, Durham, celebrating their new premises;

for the work of the Wesley Study Centre in preparing ordained and lay people to share in the ministry of Christ.

Pray for conversations in rural circuits seeking to find a way of working more closely with our ecumenical partners, particularly between the Swaledale Circuit and the Richmond Anglican Deanery and the Wensleydale Circuit and Deanery; for those working with people seeking asylum on Teeside; for our Superintendents and circuit stewards, that they may be strengthened to lead their people in the service of God's Kingdom rather than simply keep their churches going.

Darlington District

Chair:
Graham Carter

Secretary:
Paul Wood

God of all,
when I think I have all the answers,
remind me of the questions I have overlooked;
when I can't find any answers,
help me to know that the journeying is as important
as the journey's end;
and when I want to remain comfortable in my ignorance,
challenge my complacency with the mystery of your love
for this complex world;
in the name of him who died on the cross
and changed the world. Amen

Graham Carter

Give thanks for the truths God has enabled humanity to discover

day 14

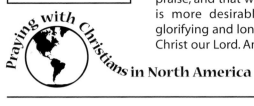

Praying with Christians in North America

Increase your grace in us, O Lord, that we may fear your Name beyond which nothing is more holy; that we may love you, beyond whom nothing is more loveable; that we may glorify you beyond whom nothing is more worthy of praise, and that we may long for you beyond whom nothing is more desirable; and grant that thus fearing, loving, glorifying and longing we may see you, face to face; through Christ our Lord. Amen

Desiderius Erasmus, 1466-1536

United Methodist Church
(USA)

Ecumenical Officer to the Council of Bishops:
Sharon Zimmerman Rader

Give thanks for prophetic voices questioning US actions and its image in world politics;
for the ministry and witness of Methodism through the African Episcopal Church, the African Methodist Episcopal Zion Church, the Christian Methodist Church and the United Methodist Church and for all that binds them together.
Pray for the President of the US and those involved in decision making as they consider the consequences of every initiative;
for Churches coping with rapid change and declining membership; for sensitive debate where there are strong differences over contemporary issues;
for deepening fellowship with indigenous communities and the wider network of relationships with members in Africa and the Caribbean.

The United Church of Canada

Acting General Secretary:
James Sinclair

Give thanks for the width of ministry carried out by the United Church with native congregations, rural and urban work, alienated young people, people with addiction problems and released prisoners.
Pray that we may learn from its long experience of being a United Church.

You have come from afar
and waited long and are wearied:
Let us sit side by side
sharing the same bread drawn from the same source
to quiet the same hunger that makes us weak.
Then standing together
let us share the same spirit, the same thoughts
that once again draw us together in friendship and unity
and peace.

Prières d'Ozawamick, Canadian Indian Liturgical text
Source Unknown

We give thanks for the faithfulness of those within our churches – both small and not so small – in maintaining a viable witness.

We pray for the many taking up new posts within the District this year and our hopes for greater networking and closer involvement between ourselves and with ecumenical partners.

Let us pray for our church and its congregation:
that we may be prepared to stand up
for people who have no voice or influence in society,
for marginalised and vulnerable people;
that we may be willing to spend time and money
to help people who are struggling with life,
who are addicted to drugs or without a home;
that we may learn to raise our voices for God's creation,
to protect it from the destruction and exploitation
that satisfy our 'comfort needs', or our greed.

Frank and Gabi Aichele, WCBP Germany/Woodbridge, Suffolk

East Anglia District

Chair:
Graham Thompson

Secretary:
Grahame Lindsay

Mission Partners:
Frankº and Gabi Aichele (Germany)

'You and I are made for goodness, for love, for transcendence, for togetherness. God has a dream that we, God's children, will come to realise that we are indeed sisters and brothers, members of one family, the human family – that all belong, all white, black, and yellow, rich and poor, beautiful and not so beautiful, young and old, male and female. There are no outsiders, all are insiders – gay and straight, Christians, Muslims, Jews, Arabs, Americans, Protestants, Roman Catholics, Afghans – all belong. And God says:"I have no one to help me realise my dream except you – will you help me?"'

Desmond Tutu, addressing Georgetown University, Washington, USA

Lord Jesus Christ,
you brought us to new birth;
you nurture and sustain us every day;
you promise to be with us tomorrow;
we give you our all.
We look to you that we might
walk only in your ways;
live in your love
and share you with all whom we meet. Amen

Graham Thompson

Give thanks for the intercession of Christ in heaven

Asia

Secretary for Asia and the Pacific:
Christine Elliott-Hall

Michael Paw Htun, Scholarship student from Burma, 2002/3

Homes in Hong Kong

If you would be the light
You must endure the burning.

Ed de la Torre, the Philippines

'May God in his grace make us the salt of the earth.'

Bishop Mondal, Bangladesh

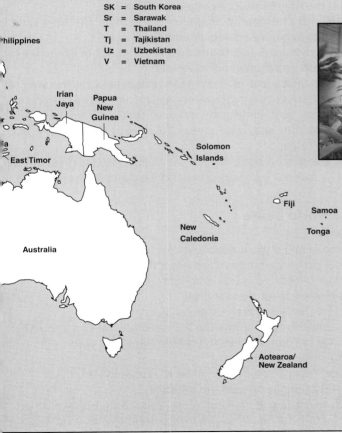

NK

SK

Japan

Af	=	Afghanistan
B	=	Bangladesh
Bh	=	Bhutan
Br	=	Brunei
K	=	Kampuchea
Ky	=	Kyrgyzstan
My	=	Myanmar
N	=	Nepal
NK	=	North Korea
L	=	Laos
Sb	=	Sabah
SK	=	South Korea
Sr	=	Sarawak
T	=	Thailand
Tj	=	Tajikistan
Uz	=	Uzbekistan
V	=	Vietnam

Philippines

Irian Jaya

Papua New Guinea

Solomon Islands

East Timor

Fiji

Samoa

New Caledonia

Tonga

Australia

Aotearoa/ New Zealand

Meeting in Tonga

'Alifelete Mone, Tonga

day 15

Take from me, O Lord, all desire for worldly praise and all uncontrolled anger and remorse. Give to me a humble and lowly heart, and a mind tender with kindness and compassion. Grant to me also, good Lord, fullness of faith, firmness of hope and fervency of love, that my one desire may be conformity to your gracious will; through Christ our Lord. Amen

Thomas More, 1478-1535

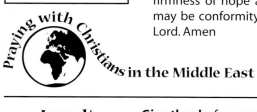

Praying with Christians in the Middle East

Israel/ Palestine

Ecumenical Accompaniment Programme in Palestine and Israel (EAPPI):
David Rowland
Brian Shackleton

Jordan

Lebanon

Give thanks for courageous Israelis and Palestinians who work against all odds to speak out against the injustices of the current situation in the Holy Land and who work in practical ways for reconciliation and hope.

There is concern about the number of Christians migrating from the Holy Land, especially since 2000.

Pray with Christian communities throughout the Holy Land, aware of being a vulnerable minority:
for all who serve with the Middle East Council of Churches as mediators and human rights workers;
for Palestinians cut off from other Palestinians by the wall of separation and from their water supply, medical aid and daily work;
for Israeli and Palestinian leaders that with wisdom and restraint they may find a way to co-exist in harmony and mutual respect;
that peoples on both sides of the 'Wall of hate' may be driven not by fear but by compassion and the desire to live in peace.

For world peace

God our Father,
as the rainbow spans the heavens when the sky is dark,
so our strife and enmities stand under the judgement and promise of your over-arching love and righteousness.
We praise you for signs of hope
and for the fact that enemies can become friends.
As your Holy Spirit draws the scattered flock of Christ together
so may the nations find a unity that eliminates war.
Help all who look to Christ
to identify the common enemies of humanity –
poverty, hunger, disease and injustice –
and work to create the structures of peace, for his sake. Amen

Kenneth Greet, Methodist Peace Fellowship

Please pray for the work towards nominating a new Chair of District for 2006-2012 and the preparatory review of the District Mission Policy Statement currently called 'What Methodism on the Isle of Man seeks to do';
for the new minister in Douglas, David Shirtliff and family;
for the expanding work of the Manx Live at Home Schemes in association with MHA;
for the ongoing work of Malcolm Peacock as Prison Chaplain.

Isle of Man District
Rheynn Ellan Vannin Yn Agglish Haasilagh

Chair:
Stephen Caddy

Secretary:
Malcolm Peacock

Prisoners of Conscience

Imagine yourself in their place:
you are in a small, dark, cold, room, or a suffocatingly hot one;
perhaps alone in empty silence,
or incarcerated with others coughing, moaning, swearing, crying ...
stiff from lack of exercise, desperately tired from lack of sleep;
the stench is overpowering, you are unwashed, your mouth is dry, your stomach gnaws with hunger ...
you are in pain because of illness or torture.
How long have you been here? Days? Months? There's no way of knowing. No news of home – no hope of release ...

Take our thoughts, Lord,
and by the power of your Holy Spirit spur us into action.
Speak to us and draw us into a deeper commitment,
that through the offering of our time, prayer and resources,
we may bring comfort, hope and release,
in the name of Christ. Amen

Olive Wimble, Amnesty International Support Group,
Highams Park, London

Pray for this and other groups who write letters and take action on behalf of those who are unjustly detained.
Amnesty International, 99-119, Rosebery Avenue, London EC1R 4RE

AMNESTY
INTERNATIONAL
UNITED KINGDOM

Looking to Christ, I see amazing grace,
generous love, restoring power, acceptance,
challenge combined with compassion,
and expectancy that I will work with him.
May the grace of Christ fill my life, my home, my work, this day,
and may your world be filled with
the amazing possibilities of grace, now and for ever. Amen

Susan Johnson, Mission Education Co-ordinator

Give thanks for the joy of human love and friendship

day 16

Dispel, O Lord, O Father of lights, all clouds of doubt, and the darkness about our earthly course, that in your light we may see light, and come both to know you as we are known, and to love you as we are loved; through Jesus Christ our Lord. Amen

Eric Milner-White, 1884-1961

Praying with Christians **in the Indian Subcontinent**

Church of Pakistan

Moderator:
Alexander Malik

Give thanks for Christians facing enormous challenges with courage and hope.

Pray for Christians who suffer discrimination in the job market, poor educational opportunities, but who find it all too easy to be drawn into crime (Christians are found in Pakistan's jails);

for centres in Islamabad and in Karachi which are working with young adults to help them overcome drug dependency;

for a group of women in Lahore supporting families and encouraging women and girls to leave the sex trade;

for ministry to people in the NW Frontier Province where Afghan refugees take shelter in transit camps and where there is a daily fear of Al Qaeda activity.

Church of Bangladesh

Moderator:
Michael Baroi

Mission Partners:
sd   James Pender
n   Gillian Rose
th/ad+ Andrew and
     Rosemary Symonds
(all joint appointments
with CofS, CMS, USPG)

Give thanks for the Church's extensive programme of work among the poorest of the poor.

Pray for the development of vocational training, centres for street children and an at-risk centre for girls who have suffered sexual abuse;

for the Government and all in authority that they may have the will to care for the 95% of people who are desperately poor.

O compassionate God,
help us to see the people around us
not from our own self-seeking perspective
but with your eyes of mercy and love.
Help us to consider people in their true humanity
so that – whether they be day labourers, rickshaw drivers,
street children, beggars or rich –
we may look with your compassion
and seek to bring your reconciling love to this broken
but beautiful world.

Michael Baroi

Give thanks for the rebuilding of Jennymount Church after the fire.

Pray for the reshaping of churches and circuits to prepare for future mission;

for a resolution of the problem of paramilitary organised crime remaining from the troubled years.

Belfast District

Superintendent:
Ivan McElhinney

Secretary:
Donald Ker

Give thanks for the growing relationship between the District and the Diocese of Ripon and Leeds, and for the new opportunities in mission which it will create.

Pray for Anglican clergy who have been given 'Authority to Minister' status within Methodist circuits and for Methodist ministers who have the Bishop's permission to officiate in Anglican churches;

for John Packer, Bishop of Ripon and Leeds, and for the new Bishop of Knaresborough, James Bell, who has special responsibilities for rural mission.

Leeds District

Chair:
Michael Townsend

Secretary:
Richard Oldroyd

Mission Partners:
Daniel° and Laura Williams, Danny, Debbie and Damaris (Cuba)

God of all grace,
you call us into new relationships of faith and love.
May we learn to trust one another
and look to Christ together,
so that the world may believe in you;
through Jesus Christ our Lord. Amen

Michael Townsend

For young people

Loving Father,
help us to encourage the full participation
    of young people
in our communities and churches.
Raise up from us a new generation of inclusiveness and respect
so that every member of our society may feel loved and valued.
Empower and equip young people
and help us to be open and ready for new experiences
as we share with men, women, boys and girls of all ages.
Unite us as the body of Christ
and may your Kingdom come in your Church.
In the power of the Holy Spirit we pray. Amen

Rachel Appleyard – MAYC staff

Amelia Trust Farm

Give thanks for our families and friends

41

day 17

Let your love fall upon the altar of our hearts, O Lord, as fire from heaven. Teach us to guard and cherish its holy flame. Strengthen our souls and kindle your love within our cold hearts that we may walk before you as pilgrims eager to reach their celestial home; through Christ our Lord. Amen

Gerhard Teersteegen, 1697-1769

 in India

---

Church of North India (CNI)

Moderator:
James Terom

Church of South India (CSI)

Moderator:
Peter Sugander

Give thanks for a Christian presence in many villages throughout India and for the many areas where Christians and Hindus live side by side and work together for the good of all.

HIV/AIDS is spreading rapidly and becoming a major problem, resulting in stigma and discrimination for many. **Pray** with all in the CNI and CSI who are equipping themselves to offer counselling, support and care.

Pray for Sudipta Singh (NMA), helping to equip dioceses and organisations of the CNI to understand and engage in holistic mission and for Vivek Samuel Masih (NMA), Mission Enabler for Youth Action in Development – helping unemployed young people in slum areas such as Dakshinpuri and Khanpur.

Pray with the CSI for its 10-year Campaign for the rights of the girl-child. 25% girls do not reach their 15th birthday; many are killed in infancy. The CSI seeks to encourage people to respect the rights of all children and to help girls to overcome the problems of their social background and to develop self-esteem.

Pray for Dalits struggling against those who want to retain the caste-system as cheap labour;

for farmers in Kerala whose prices for tea and coffee have been forced down by transnational companies.

Loving and sustaining God,
giver of life and rebuker of all that discriminates,
we pray that all racial, religious and economic discrimination,
which cause hatred, violence and civil war,
may be washed away by the power of your love and peace.
We pray for your Church
that it may continue to witness to your justice and harmony
in all these situations.
In the name of Jesus Christ your Son. Amen

Sanjiv Christian, Gujarat, North India, student at the UCA

Give thanks for the recent covenant of Churches Together in all Lincolnshire.

Pray for us as we work together in local communities:
> in proclaiming the good news and nurturing new believers;
> in expressing the love of God through common service;
> in resisting and seeking to transform all that threatens or subverts the values of the Kingdom;
> in promoting justice, peace and reconciliation;
> in celebrating and preserving the integrity of creation;
> in finding other partners with whom we can work.

Lincoln and Grimsby District

Chair:
David Perry

Secretary:
Mark Childs

Faith and knowledge

Loving God, our heavenly teacher,
source of our faith and our knowledge,
give us your wisdom to measure our faith and think accordingly.
When we see only the puzzling reflections of your truth,
let us long to see your face.
When we realise that our knowledge is only partial
give us clarity of thought
and encourage us to move on to know more.
Give us courage to say what we know
and humility to admit our ignorance.
Fill us with your discerning Spirit
to distinguish between faith and familiarity.
Remind us that love is the greatest of all gifts,
through the One who lived in perfect love:
Jesus Christ our Lord. Amen

Israel Selvanayagam, Principal of the UCA

When I'm tired and out of patience,
I look to Christ who accepts me with his love:
when my brain is stressed and chasing round in circles,
I look to Christ to calm me with his peace:
when I feel weighed down by all life's pain and struggles,
I look to Christ to renew me with his joy.

Today, I will look to Christ instead of myself –
his strength will carry me –
his grace will be sufficient for all my needs.
Thanks be to God.

Elizabeth Rundle, London Forest

Give thanks for the peace of God which passes all understanding

day 18

Love of the heart of Jesus, inflame me; strength of the heart of Jesus, uphold me; wisdom of the heart of Jesus, teach me; will of the heart of Jesus guide me; zeal of the heart of Jesus, consume me.

St. John Eudes, 1601-1680

Praying with Christians **in Asia (1)**

Myanmar/ Burma
The Methodist Church of Upper Myanmar

Methodist President:
C Kapa

Give thanks for people of faith and hope.

Pray with all who serve and witness in very difficult situations and who long for freedom and democracy. Genocide continues against Burma's ethnic minorities. Whole villages are destroyed, and there is looting, torture, rape and murder. Thousands continue to be driven out of their country and many live in camps on the border with Thailand. Many of these are destitute children, disabled and confused. Pray for those who work with them and for all who risk their lives in responding to desperate situations.

Saving God, whose activity is seen in the rise and fall of nations,
we pray with the people of Burma,
knowing that their struggle is your struggle,
and that evil cannot prevail for ever.
And so we pray that more just ways may emerge
so that peace may come without violence.

Nepal
The United Mission to Nepal (UMN)

Director of the UMN:
Jennie Collins

Mission Partners:
ad/n   Paul and Sarah
   Wright,
   Jack and Asha
ad/ad Michael and
   Maureen
   Hawksworth
t/ed   Allan and
   Andrea Smith (+CA)

Give thanks that the UMN can, with joy, celebrate 50 years' work in Nepal and for the changes that have been wrought in many people's lives and in the lives of whole communities.

Pray for the Mission as it moves forward into a period of change: that the right decisions be taken about new areas of work and the appointment of staff to new positions;
for the changing unstable political situation – that both Maoists and Security Forces act with restraint and political leaders with wisdom, so that the peace we all long for may be achieved.

Elizabeth Barrie, UMN

Do not look forward to the changes and chances of this life in fear; rather look to them full of hope that, as they arise, God will deliver you out of them. He has kept you hitherto. Do you but hold fast to his dear hand, and he will lead you safely through all things, and, when you cannot stand, he will bear you in his arms.

St. Francis de Sales (1567-1622)

Give thanks for the appointment of a personal development facilitator, based in the city centre, to work with survivors of sexual abuse.

Please pray for us as we explore, within the District and with our partner Churches, how together we can better serve this region in mission;

for those churches and circuits working through the joy and pain of change to discover new ways of being the Church where they are.

Liverpool District

Chair:
James Booth

Secretary:
Deacon Ronnie Aitchison

Living Lord, your love lies at the heart of all creation.
We give you thanks for the vibrancy and diversity
that we see when we open our eyes to your world.
Help us to see you in others,
to accept others as they are and where they are,
as you do,
that, through us and our service of you,
your Kingdom may come;
through Jesus Christ, our Lord. Amen

Jim Booth

The face of Christ

Loving God, where do we see the face of Christ in our world?
  Can we see Christ in the brokenness of humanity?
  Can we accept Christ of the shadows?
  Can we allow ourselves to be fragile and see him that way?
  Lord, help us.
  Can we see Christ in the wealth of society?
  Can we accept Christ of the neon lights?
  Can we allow ourselves to be robust and see him that way?
  Lord, help us.
  Thank you, God of all,
        for being with us in our own contradictions.
  Help us to be open to your overwhelming presence
        to begin to understand deep contentment,
        nothing lacking,
        fullness,
        bliss. Amen

Christine Elliott-Hall, Area Secretary for Asia and the Pacific

Give thanks for our share in Christ's ministry of reconciliation

day 19

Praying with Christians in Asia (2)

Deliver us, O Lord, from a deceitful heart. Forgive, we pray, the barbed word deliberately spoken; the thoughtless word hastily said and the envious look furtively cast. Forgive the ear rejoicing in the news of another's downfall; the feet loitering in forbidden paths and the grasping hand reaching out for personal gain; and all for the sake of Christ our Lord. Amen

John Baillie, 1886-1960

Sri Lanka

Methodist President:
Noel Fernando

Mission Partners:
lib Margaret (née Julian) and Kithiri Mudalige and Nathan (+USPG)
p/m David° and Sue Palmer

Give thanks for places which were once 'no man's land' where Tamils and Sinhalese are now cultivating the land together and have formed a peace association.

Pray for those who face danger in working for reconciliation;
for inter-faith nurseries where children learn to respect each other's traditions;
for the healing of bitter memories between Buddhists and Hindus;
for all people of goodwill who seek to live together in harmony;
for the Peace Process: that the very fragile work of reconciliation may continue and bring a more lasting peace;
for Church leaders in this context and for all who seek to express the love of Christ to care for refugees and those whose homes were destroyed in the conflict.

Indonesia and East Timor

Gereja Methodista Bishop:
R T Tambunan

Mission Partner:
sp/ag Peter Storey

Give thanks for the formation of the Episcopal Area of the Methodist Church in Indonesia since 2001, for church growth and enthusiasm to spread the gospel in Indonesia.

Pray for the political situation that peace may be sustained;
for the developing of good relationships between Christians, Muslims, Buddhists and Hindus;
for religious freedom, and for our working together to overcome violence and terrorist threats;
for economic growth to reduce the number of jobless people, starvation, crime and poverty;
for the GMI Mission of 2010 with the hope that by then we will have congregations in 33 provinces: our motto is 'In The Unity of the Holy Spirit to Serve The Nation';
for the 100th Anniversary of our GMI Mission in Indonesia in May 2005.

R T Tambunan

Give thanks for training opportunities at Hartley Victoria College and the Partnership for Theological Education; for new initiatives through the Manchester Centre for Public Theology.

Pray for the District Mission Enablers and the Training and Development Officer as they work with the new District Chair to help the circuits; for increasing co-operation with Anglican colleagues in the Manchester, Chester and Derby Dioceses in consultation with other ecumenical partners.

Manchester and Stockport District

Chair:
Keith Davies

Secretary:
Frederick Bell

Sometimes it's hard

Lord, with every news item, the world seems more in a mess
and I don't know where to start.
With every trip to church I seem to loathe how comfortable
and upright we all are.
Why can't we admit that we don't have it sorted?

Remind me that 'uncomfortable' does not always mean wrong,
and that your love is found in the most unusual places.
Let us recognise our gifts, believe in ourselves,
and use them as opportunities to serve you.
Make me never too proud to ask for help.

Show me how to engage with the world
and then simply give me the strength to keep on living,
so that day by day, as an example to others,
we can all make a difference and pass on the overwhelming joy
of feeling what it is to be loved. Amen

Chris Cornell, Methodist Youth President

Loving Father,
with a motherly heart you come to those who starve.
We praise you.
We thank you for people who give sacrificially
while they live in the midst of those who exploit the poor.
Thank you for teaching us the values of the Kingdom
through the poor who willingly share
what they have with others.
Give us the mind and strength to do the same;
in the name of your Son Jesus. Amen

Samuel Singh, South India, student at the UCA

Give thanks for all who are agents of Christ's compassion

47

day 20

Gracious God, look upon a sinner who is yet created in your image. Look upon a disciple into whose heart you gaze. Look upon a child who longs to love you with a heart yet more perfect, and looking, forgive, and gazing, pardon and bless; for your truth and your mercy's sake. Amen

François Fenelon, 1651-1715

 in Asia (3)

Singapore

Methodist Bishop:
Robert Solomon

We give thanks for continuing political stability and social and religious harmony in our country.

We pray for the 8th General Conference of the Methodist Church in Singapore, 18-23 October 2004;

for the launch of Mission in Thailand, and the ordination of Thai pastors later in the year;

for peace, racial and religious harmony;

for the Singapore Methodist Missions Society and our missionaries;

for the work of the Methodist Welfare Services, the social arm of the Methodist Church in Singapore.

Robert Solomon

Malaysia

Methodist Bishop:
Peter Chio Sing Ching

Special assignment:
th   David and Rhona Burfield

We give thanks for the harmony and peace that we experience as a multi-racial nation and for developments in our economic, social and political life.

We pray that God will continue to bless this country and anoint our government with wisdom and understanding to sustain political and financial stability. We pray for unity between Christian denominations so that together they may spread the good news throughout Malaysia. Lord, protect our churches from materialistic influences and help us to be more sensitive towards people in need: to love others as you love us, and give us strength and courage to overcome our weakness.

We pray for our young people for the sake of the future and for our educational system, that every student may benefit from it. We pray for all who are sick, in sorrow, or lonely, that they will know that your comfort and grace will always be with them. In your precious name we pray. Amen

Jessica Balaya (Malaysian Student at Methodist International House, Bristol)

Give thanks for an ecumenical area established with the United Reformed Church in South East Northumberland.

Please pray for Steve Lindridge, our newly appointed District Evangelism Enabler, and all who serve in the District as chaplains, especially Andrew Letby in his new responsibilities as Workplace Chaplain and Economic Affairs Field Officer; for the Diakonia 19th World Assembly taking place in our region next July.

Your street

Hold before God your neighbours,
others in your street or area,
and those who live around your church.
Think of them in their different situations.
Whatever you know of them, imagine yourself 'in their shoes'
  and draw them into the light of God's presence.

> Living God,
> we pray for our community,
> that in its homes and streets
> people may hear your voice.
> In their longing to be loved and valued,
> may they learn that you have always been there,
> patiently waiting for us all to turn to you
> in faith and love
> to receive the new life you give
> through your Son, Jesus Christ. Amen

Maureen Edwards

Newcastle upon Tyne District

Chair:
Leo Osborn

Secretary:
Elizabeth Edwards

Mission Partners:
Sipho° and Zime Nyembezi, Nkululeko, Nondumiso, Nosipho and Nokwazi (MCSA) Hendry° and Rita Ponniah, Joshua, Ruth and Roy (Malaysia)

 Lord Christ,
all creation looks to you, its life-giver and sustainer.
Your Church looks to you, its way, its truth, its life.
Your needy world looks to you, bread of life and living water.
As we look to you we find you looking on us with love.
Help us always to look on others with that same love,
for your name's sake. Amen

Leo Osborn

Give thanks for all opportunities to proclaim the gospel

day 21

O Lord my God, I adore you as my first beginning and I long for you as my last end. Conduct me, therefore, O gracious Lord, by your wisdom. Restrain me with your justice, comfort me with your mercy, and defend me with your power; and of your love, enlighten my understanding, enflame my will and purify my soul; for Jesu's sake. Amen

Richard Challoner, 1691-1781

Praying with Christians in the Far East (1)

China

President of China Christian Council:
Cao Shengjie

Amity teachers:
Janet Dickinson
Mick and Anne Kavanagh
Kate Keir
Jody and Michelle Marshall
Matthew Sydall
Joanna White

Amity is a Chinese non-Government Organisation founded by Christians

Give thanks for exchanges of personnel between congregations in Hong Kong and mainland **China** and the enrichment of mind and spirit which they engender;
for practical help given by the Churches during the SARS epidemic in the spring of 2003.
Pray for Amity teachers seeking to share their faith in mainland China, not through open evangelism – which is forbidden – but by the quality of their lives and teaching;
for the Amity Grandma project which recruits retired doctors and teachers to provide support and care for orphans;
for projects enabling over 50,000 school dropouts to continue their education;
for their rural development projects, promoting sustainable development work to provide poor, remote villages with food, water, vegetation and alternative energy sources;
for the work of the China Christian Council in hospitals and clinics, homes for older people, kindergartens and other projects;
for all that the CCC is doing to respond to China's immense social challenges – especially the rapid spread of HIV/AIDS – and to show the love of Christ in action.

Hong Kong
(Special Administrative Region of China)

Methodist President:
Ralph Lee

Amity HK:
Ian Groves

Dear Lord, we pray for **Hong Kong**. You have blessed us as we have grown from a remote fishing village into a large metropolitan city. Today, Hong Kong is undergoing economic restructuring and the disparity between rich and poor is widening; it is bombarded by debates about social issues and political development ...
Lord, strengthen your people. Give us perseverance, wisdom and loving hearts. May the Church be the light and salt of society. Give us faith and courage to know that, as we follow your teaching and accept your guidance, a just, participatory and healthy society can be built.

Katherine Ng, Hong Kong

Give thanks for the continuing growth of Trinity Church, Lisburn, and for the completion of their large extension; for a number of circuits undertaking building schemes; for the stories of people coming to faith.

Pray for the new District Superintendent, Kenneth Todd; for the circuits as they begin to implement the 'Connexion Report'; for all who work with young people and children.

Down District

Superintendent:
Kenneth Todd

Secretary:
Thomas McKnight

Give thanks for Christchurch, the newly built Methodist and Roman Catholic Church in Nelson, as it becomes a powerful symbol of hope for Christian unity and building bridges within the community of this former mill town.

Pray for all who are beginning to take the risk of mission within their communities: for the basement project with children and young people in Burnley and the plans for a non-alcoholic bar as a safe place in this centre of east Lancashire night life; for the new Anglican/Methodist faith community which is ministering in new ways on the Grange Park estate, a very needy area of Blackpool; for the Churches Together ministry among asylum seekers and refugees in Blackburn and Darwen.

North Lancashire District

Chair:
Stephen Poxon

Secretary:
Andrew Horsfall

I look to Christ this day
for strength in my weakness,
for healing in my sickness.

I look to Christ this day
for hope in my despair,
for love in my hatred.

I look to Christ this day
for peace in my restlessness,
for forgiveness in my sin.

I look to Christ this day
for fullness in my emptiness,
for life in my death.

I look to Christ this day
and pray that Christ will look upon me.

Stephen Poxon

Give thanks for the presence and power of the Holy Spirit

day 22

Grant to us, O Lord, ears to hear your voice, eyes to see your beauty, wills to obey your commandments, and hearts to love your name, so that hearing, seeing, obeying and loving we may come at last to the joys of your Kingdom; through Christ our Lord. Amen

Christina Rossetti, 1830-1885

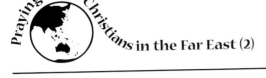 **in the Far East (2)**

Korea

Presiding Bishop:
Kwang Young

Give thanks for Christian congregations, large and small.
Pray for new converts and those who care for them that their faith may grow and be deepened;
for dialogue between people of different faiths;
for discernment in coping with change in all areas of Korean life;
for reconciliation between North and South;
for all who are victims of arbitrary executions and torture (there are tens of thousands of prisoners in North Korea) and for torturers who are trained not to see prisoners as human beings.

Japan

General Secretary of the Kyodan, the United Church of Christ in Japan:
Shiro Harada

Mission Partners:
ed David and Keiko Gray, Elizabeth and Paul
ed Sheila Norris
ed Daniel and Yasuko Dellming, Momoko and Daisuke

Give thanks that the Kyodan is now able to send Mission Partners to other countries.
Pray for Christians who teach in schools and universities that through their daily witness and lifestyle, young people may become aware of God's presence and the challenge of the gospel;
for small Christian groups who meet for Bible study and prayer, asking that their weakness may be turned to strength;
for the ability to transcend cultural boundaries;
for political stability and peace, and for reliance, not on military bases and armaments but upon the power of God to bring a change of heart and movement toward peace in the world.

Eternal God ...
renew our bodies as fresh as the morning flowers ...
Give us wings of freedom, like the birds in the sky
to begin a new journey.
Restore justice and freedom, as a mighty stream
running continuously as day follows day.
We thank you for the gift of this morning
and a new day to work with you.

From a prayer by Masao Takenaka – Your Will Be Done
© Christian Conference of Asia

Give thanks for the work of the 'Contagious' youth led worship based in Belper Circuit, which for the last seven years has been successful as a contemporary expression of the gospel.

Pray for the District Policy Committee as it seeks to encourage churches and circuits to work in partnership with each other and different agencies, in order to make best use of all available resources;

and for the new Stanhope Centre in Mansfield, where church and community groups work in partnership for vulnerable people.

Nottingham and Derby District

Chair:
Wesley Blakey

Secretary:
Averil George

Mission Partners:
Alexander° and Emily Siatwinda (Zambia)

Rooted, yet never still
Moss-green and grey skeletal tree
dripping with cold in wintry sky,
wrecked and worthless seemingly,
and no-one hurrying by
sees it.

Forgotten, the autumnal glow;
forgotten, leaves that shone and bled,
lining gutters under snow,
their grandeur now is dead
and gone.

Yet there's a hint of lightest green:
is that a bud blown in the wind?
Could a leaf yet still unseen
be ready to self
indicate?

This tree's whole life is constant change,
rooted in place yet never still.
Oh that I could rearrange
frail mind into bold will
for that.

Wesley Blakey

For the rich variety of responses to your love,
    we thank you, Lord.
Help us to respect ways of discipleship which
    are different from ours.
For the many different people whose insights have brought life
and hope to your Church, we thank you, Lord.
Challenge us with new vision and open our eyes to new ways
of faith and life. Amen

Richard Bielby, Shetland District

Give thanks for the ministry of the word, the sacraments and prayer

day 23

Father of all, pour into our hearts the love that casts out fear, the truth that sets us free and the grace that is sufficient for all our needs, and grant that we may evermore rejoice that though you are unseen, you are not unknown and that though you are hidden from our eyes we may behold your beauty at the last; through Christ our Lord. Amen

Louisa M Alcott, 1833-1888

Praying with Christians in Australia and New Zealand

Aotearoa/ New Zealand

Methodist President:
Lynne Frith

Give thanks for a country whose life is based on the Treaty of Waitangi, which recognises the rights of the indigenous people and provides the basis for a bi-cultural partnership.

Pray for the people of Aotearoa New Zealand:

for the Government and all members of Parliament, as they seek to order the life of the nation on the basis of the Treaty, to meet the needs of all people;

for a people grappling with the meaning of nationhood, seeking to honour their Treaty, to be free of racism, to respect each other, to value our cultural heritage and to build a caring and sensitive community.

Lynne Frith

The Uniting Church of Australia
(UCA)

President:
Dean Drayton

Give thanks that after being in dialogue since 1979, the Uniting Church has taken the first step towards union with the Anglican Church in Australia.

Pray that this may bring benefit to every local church.

Loving God,
undiminished by distance, unconstrained by place or time,
for ever seeking, for ever calling, for ever drawing humanity
to yourself and to each other,
we glimpse your Spirit
in the brooding silence of awesome landscape,
the ancient law of Aboriginal nations ...
Yet in the vastness of this place, Australia,
we often feel alone, alienated, unworthy
of more than a passing acquaintance with your love.
Help us to understand
you ever yearn to make us whole,
drawing near in Christ to show us the way. Amen

Brian Smith, Mission Prayer Handbook of the UCA

We are thankful for ways in which God is working through his people, changing lives and impacting the community.

Please pray for the vulnerable, particularly the elderly and disabled who are more and more a target for those who prey on the weak;

for an increasingly large number who have little sense of their need of God or church, and who perhaps feel that church is irrelevant.

Portadown District

Superintendent:
Maurice Laverty

Secretary:
Brian Sweeney

Give thanks for commitment to unity among those who belong to Churches Together in South Yorkshire and Churches Together in Nottinghamshire and Derbyshire, and pray for their respective Ecumenical Officers, Louise Dawson and Philip Webb; for the commitment to unity of all our church leaders and especially for Jack Nicholls – Bishop of Sheffield, George Cassidy – Bishop of Southwell and Jonathan Bailey – Bishop of Derby.

Pray that those who seek a new purpose and direction for their lives will look to Christ today and receive his guidance;

that those who need forgiveness for hurting others will look to Christ today and feel his love;

that those who want the unity of the Church and peace in the world will look to Christ today, and in his Spirit knock down dividing walls of hostility, build bridges of reconciliation, and lay foundations of togetherness.

Sheffield District

Chair:
David Halstead

Secretary:
Gillian Newton

Mission Partners:
Jonathan° and Elizabeth Gichaara, Neene, Israel and Muthomi (Kenya)

Almighty God,
in the sandy deserts of Africa, the white snows of Europe
and the gushing waters of the Victoria Falls,
we glorify your name.
When we look at the seas, the high mountains,
and in the sweet face of a new born baby…
we see an awesome God.
Father, Son and Holy Spirit, in your oneness,
teach us to live in harmony:
husband and wife, poor and rich,
black and white, Muslim and Jew…
all created in your image and Jesus died so that we may live.
Send your prophetic Church into this divided world
to proclaim unity in Christ Jesus. Amen

Edson and Sammie Dube, WCBP Zimbabwe/S Wales

Give thanks for unity, God's will and gift to the Church

Europe

Secretary for Europe:
Colin Ride

God is weak and powerless in the world, and that is exactly the way, the only way, in which he can be with us and help us.

*Dietrich Bonhoeffer
(1906-1945)*

*Balloons saying
'No to neonazis'*

Ireland

Al = Albania
Au = Austria
B = Belgium
Bo = Bosnia-Herzegovina
Cr = Croatia
Cz = Czech Republic
E = Estonia
G = Gibraltar
Gr = Greece
H = Hungary
L = Latvia
Li = Lithuania
Lu = Luxembourg
M = Moldavia
Mc = Macedonia
Mn = Montenegro
Sb = Serbia
Sl = Slovak Republic
Sn = Slovenia
Sw = Switzerland

British Methodist Districts

- dots are major towns and cities
- numbers correspond to the day in the Prayer Handbook

30 Orkney

Shetland

30

20

9

13

15

27

16

29

21

18 6

19

25

17

8

11

22

28

23

14

8

5

8

2

1

7

24

26

3

4

12

10
Channel Islands

Isles of Scilly

Methodists for World Mission (MWM) at Sidholme 2003

Students of Methodist International House, Bristol

day 26

Praying with Christians in Europe (1)

Lord, I bring the poverty of my soul to be transformed by your beauty; the wildness of my passions to be tamed by your love; the stubbornness of my will to be conformed to your commandments and the yearnings of my heart to be renewed by your grace; both now and for ever. Amen

Catherine of Genoa, 1447-1510

The United Methodist Northern Europe Central Conference

Bishop: Öystein Olsen

Superintendents:

Norway: Ola Westad, Vidar Sten Bjerkseth

Sweden: Anders Svensson, Peter Svanberg, Solveig Högberg, Bimbi Ollberg

Denmark: Christian Alsted, Keld Munk

Finland *(Swedish language)* Hans Vaxby, Fredrik Wegelius

Finland *(Finnish language)* Timo Virtanen

Estonia: Olav Pärnamets

Latvia: Arijs Viksna

Lithuania: Chet Cataldo

Russia
Bishop of the UMC in Eurasia: Rüdiger Minor

Mission Partner:
p Nicola Vidamour°

The Conference of European Churches
General Secretary:
Keith Clements

Give thanks that in the last decade 20% of Russians have moved from atheism to the Christian faith, and that religious freedom is written into the Constitution.

Christ, when we look to you we see calmness and confidence, hope and love, forgiveness and healing.
We give thanks that the lives of so many adults and children in Russia have been transformed by the freedom to look to you and read your word.
We pray for grace to look to you as one who unites people of different confessions and cultures in the name of the Father, the Son and the Holy Spirit. Amen

Nicola Vidamour and the Pskov English Club

Pray for the Church in **Russia** as it seeks to respond to the challenges of deep secularisation, widespread poverty, low birth rates, poor health and the spread of HIV/AIDS (the population has declined by 2% since 1992);
for the building of a multi-cultural nation;
for political wisdom and economic stability;
that religious freedom may continue.

Pray for renewed vision for the Church in **Sweden** and for their continuing reflection on the mission and ministry of the Church;
for the working out of their new plan 'The Task' (based on 'Our Calling') to help local congregations to determine priorities;
for the work of the Baltic Mission Theological Seminary in **Estonia**, for students engaged there in full-time or distance learning and for the College's influence throughout the country;
for congregations in **Latvia**, for the healing of bitter memories of past events and for people who are marginalised by economic growth.

We give thanks for the opening of the new Broadstone Methodist Church building, and the completion of other major building schemes in the District;

for the initiation of many new parallel congregations and alternative acts of worship;

for the increasing growth in confidence and the willingness of some congregations to take risks of faith.

We pray for a deepening experience of God and the recovery of an ability to have meaningful conversations about Jesus Christ with the people who come onto our church premises;

for the work of Sarum College and the District 'Bread and Butter' study programmes designed to extend and deepen our witness to the gospel;

for the Chaplains to the Forces and for the work of District Chaplains in Business, Industry and Commerce;

for the building and completion of the new Emmanuel Church in Reading.

Southampton District

Chair:
Tom Stuckey

Secretary:
David Hinchliffe

Almighty God, we praise you for the men and women you have sent in days past to call the Church to its tasks and to renew its life. Raise up in our day teachers and prophets inspired by your Spirit, whose voices will give strength to your Church and proclaim the reality of your Kingdom. Amen

Prayer from Denmark

Look to Christ?

Why should I look to Christ?
  I am satisfied with my life; he will disturb it.
  I am happy in my church; he will change it.
  I am content in my world; he will shatter it.
  I have what I want; he will tell me what I need.
For his world is larger than mine.
  He reaches out to those who are unsatisfied.
  He passes judgement on the complacent.
  He penetrates the pain of a wounded world.
  He calls us to embrace those who have nothing.
Should I look to Christ?
  I must!

Tom Stuckey

Give thanks for the suffering and victory of Jesus Christ

day 27

O blessed Jesus, immortal and victorious, by the sorrow you suffered when all the powers of your heart failed you, have mercy on us and help us in our days of darkness and in our hours of weakness, that we do not lose hold of you either in this life, or in the life of the world to come; and this we ask for your own name's sake. Amen

St. Bridget of Sweden, 1303-1373

in Europe (2)

Belgium

President of the Eglise Protestante Unie:
Daniel Vanescote

We thank God for 25 years as the United Protestant Church in Belgium. We look to Christ with gratitude for the men and women who have been called to be pastors and leaders in his Church.
We pray to God to support us when we are asked to give reasons for the hope that is in us, especially in the growing inter-cultural context of our country.

Daniel Vanescote

The United Methodist German Central Conference

Bishop:
Walter Klaiber

Mission Partners:
p   Barry° and Gillian Sloan, Michael and Megan
p   Vanessa Cook

Give thanks for the publication of a new hymnal and for an increase in membership due particularly to fast-growing Ghanaian congregations in Hamburg, Dusseldorf and Essen.
Pray with the Methodist Church as it reduces the number of pastors in its struggle with financial problems;
for work with young people;
for the Ecumenical Kirchentag in Berlin that its witness in unity may inspire greater ecumenism throughout Germany;
for relationships between Churches of different traditions throughout Europe: that the principles of *Charta Oecumenica* may draw Christians together.

Our good God, we thank you for all possibilities we have to share the good news of your love in Jesus Christ with other people.
Help us that we become more open and more able to reach out to them. Make us ready to share our lives and our goods with them and let them realise what it may mean to them to share your love with us. Amen

Walter Klaiber

We give thanks for all who are committed to celebrate God's love through worship, prayer and action. We pray that we may seek further opportunities for sharing in God's mission and that we may learn from one another.

Give thanks for all who worship and minister in our Local Ecumenical Partnerships with the United Reformed, Anglican and Baptist Churches, and for the encouragement we can give to each other as we seek the way ahead.

Pray for the establishment of the Bradford Inner Ring Group Phase 2 as a way of working ecumenically as we seek to live in our multi-faith and challenging city environment;

for the newly established District Mission Enabling Team and recruitment for a Mission Enabling Officer to begin work in 2005.

West Yorkshire District

Chair:
Peter Whittaker

Secretary:
Ruth Gee

In the storm, look to Christ – A meditation

Based on Matthew 14.25-32

We are among people thrashing about in murky water, clinging on to anything ... clinging to the boat that contains our money, possessions, our pride and human strength. Water is engulfing us, waves of doubt and despair battering us. We are worn out physically and spiritually by fierce winds blowing us this way and that ... frightened by the way the dark waters are pulling us down into nothingness.

But Jesus calls, 'It is I. Don't be afraid.' We look around for him, but – like the disciples – drift away and cannot hear him through the problems that engulf us. Our hearts are hardened, our vision dulled. Yet Jesus stands there, like a lighthouse, protecting and guiding us. He calls to us to walk with him on the water. He wants us to let go of our boats, bobbing up and down in the waves that overwhelm us, and look to him.

Look! See his calmness, reaching out his hand to lift us up. The swirling sea becomes a still, blue walkway. We see him now, amazed at what he can do for us when we let go of all that pulls us back into the destructive waters. We can move on, set sail once more on our journey of faith and hear Jesus whispering through the breeze, 'It is I. Don't be afraid.'

Peter Taylor, Bulgaria

Jesus said, 'I am the way and the truth and the life.'
Christ, we look to you:
    rescue us, renew us, restore us, resource us.
Gazing upon you, we
    follow the way,
    seek the truth
    and live the life. Amen

Peter Whittaker

Give thanks for the power of Christ to transform our suffering

day 28

Lord, teach us that your Son died to save us, not from suffering but from ourselves; not from injustice, but from being unjust; and not from dying but so that we might die to ourselves; and this we ask through the same Christ our Lord. Amen

George Macdonald, 1824-1905

 in Central Europe (1)

United Methodist Central and Southern Europe Central Conference

Bishop:
Heinrich Bolleter

Superintendents:

Algeria
Daniel Nussbaumer

Austria
Lothar Poell

Bulgaria
Bedros Altunian

Mission Partners:
sd Peter and
  Samantha Taylor

Czech Republic
Josef Cervenak

Slovak Republic
Pavel Prochazka

Hungary
Istvan Csernak

Poland
Edward Puslecki

Switzerland/France
Daniel Nussbaumer
Markus Bach
Hanna, Elsi Atorfor
  and Walter Wilhelm

Give thanks for the long history of mission work begun in **Algeria** by French Methodists in 1880, and for its continuing part in the life of the United Methodist Central Conference of Europe; for church growth in **Bulgaria** after a past history of suppression and persecution in the Communist era when only five pastors remained alive. There are now 35 congregations.

Pray for the training programme for new pastors in Graz, **Austria**;
for new churches being planted and hope for the future;
for the mission of the church in Sumen which includes a social centre and hospice (small cottage hospital);
for the life of the new church in Varne (opened in 2003).

Pray for Mariela Markova (NMA), a missionary for three Armenian congregations in **Bulgaria**;
for Sergey and Esther Bogomazuik (NMAs) in the Carpathian Ukraine, leading the church, forming cell groups and serving orphans and the poor in the community.

Pray for mission in **Hungary** among the Roma people;
for literacy work with the women and kindergartens for their children, that these women may be encouraged to achieve qualifications for future employment;
for the first Hungarian Gypsy pastor now in training;
for the growing number of Hungarian theological students;
for all who are involved in building a new church at Miskolc.

Pray for the 'Glass of Water' project in Warsaw, **Poland**, helping alcoholics and their families, and providing summer camps for children, and for the development and training of young lay leadership in Krakow, the cultural heart of Poland;
for the healing of bitter memories of the camps and the evil committed at Auschwitz in the Second World War.

Pray for people of minority faith traditions in **France**.

Give thanks for the Marches Circuit created out of three former single stations.

Pray for the development of youth work across the District; for the District project with Christian Aid, 'Building Hope' in the Gaza Strip; for churches and circuits as they address the nature of their contemporary mission.

Loving and all knowing God,
In helping others, we look to Christ.
In stepping out on behalf of the oppressed, we look to Christ.
In stepping out of our comfort zone, we look to Christ.
In working in unity with other Churches, we look to Christ.
In believing in Christ's death and resurrection,
we look to him and find him. Amen

Samantha and Peter Taylor, UMC Bulgaria

Wolverhampton and Shrewsbury District

Chair:
Peter Curry

Secretary:
Brenda Shuttleworth

Mission Partners:
Solomonaº and Ana Potogi, Lusa and Wesley (Samoa)

As we look around, we see many faces:
young and old, black and white;
some smiling, others with tears;
some with the sparkle of hope in their eyes;
others with the gloom of fear and anxiety.
In all these faces may we see your face
and rejoice in your presence with us. Amen

Peter Curry

Gracious God, whose only desire it is that men and women will come from the east and from the west, from the north and from the south and will sit down together at the feast of your Kingdom; have mercy on those of Abrahamic faith, whether they are Jews, Christians or Muslims, and grant that they may behold in you the one God and Father of all, and see in each other only those created in your own image and likeness; and that thus beholding and seeing they may turn aside from all evil and violence and, with one mind, undertake that ministry of reconciliation which you have committed to them; for to you belongs all honour, all glory and praise, now and for ever. Amen

Norman Wallwork

Give thanks for signs of renewal in the Church through the Holy Spirit

day 29

Lord, let me be yours. Let me not draw back, neither from heaven, nor from your divinity, nor from your cross. Let me be yours to whom I owe my creation and my redemption. Touch my heart and sanctify it, and consecrate me in your service, for ever. Amen

Lucy Herbert, 1669-1744

Praying with Christians in Central Europe (2)

United Methodist Central and Southern Europe Central Conference
(continued)

Serbia and Montenegro
Superintendent:
Martin Hovan

Macedonia
Superintendent:
Wilhelm Nausner

Give thanks for strength of faith and witness in difficult times.

Pray for congregations in **Serbia and Montenegro**, working to break down the barriers of suspicion between church and society and to be witnesses amid prevailing atheism;
for work in Jabuka (in spite of few resources) with Roma Gypsy children, and for the large Roma congregation there;
for the Ecumenical Humanitarian Organisation helping vulnerable people through the distribution of seeds, clothes, school equipment and baby items, and for the psycho-dynamic counselling service, laundry and other projects.

Give thanks for two small congregations in **Macedonia** working with the Roma people (since their expulsion from Kosovo in 1999) and the trust placed in them by about 700 very vulnerable people. They have no status; they are not wanted by the local population and it is impossible to guarantee their safety in Kosovo.

Pray for Katarina Nikolic (NMA – Yugoslavia), working with the Roma people in Srbabran and running evangelical and social programmes as well as weekly church services;
for Sofia Trajkovska (NMA – Macedonia), running the UMC Office and involved in social outreach;
for Mirce Tancer (NMA – Macedonia), Co-ordinator and lay preacher, serving in Monospitovo, and working with church programmes.

Remembering the deep-rooted suspicion and hatred that destroys relationships between people of different races and cultures, pray for divided communities in Europe and throughout the world;
for all who act as mediators;
for ourselves that we may be peacemakers.
Pray with the people of Macedonia who mourn the tragic loss of President Boris Trajkovski, that his successor may continue to build trust and tolerance in this turbulent Balkan region.

We celebrate and give thanks for creative property schemes, for important work among asylum seekers in Hull and for the energy and commitment of many people.
We pray for the Selby and District Regeneration Programme after the closure of the coal mines;
for our growing ecumenical relationships and for the creative partnership between the York Institute for Community Theology and the University College of York St John.

York and Hull District

Chair:
Stephen Burgess

Secretary:
Rosemary Harrison

Mission Partners:
David° and Jessie
Wee (Singapore)

Channels of healing

Father God,
once again we offer to you ourselves
as living temples of your Holy Spirit
that you may inhabit our praises today.
Give us contrite hearts,
hearts of worship, hearts of praise.
May we be touched by your presence
so that your Spirit may be seen in our lives.
Make us aware of people's suffering in our community:
the bereaved,
those who are sick in body, mind and soul,
the elderly and infirm and all who are lonely.
And, as we pray for the needs of others,
give us grace and humility
to become channels of your healing,
in the name of Jesus Christ our Lord. Amen

Maureen Thomson, Appleton Roebuck, York

Gracious God,
in our vulnerability give us strength
and in our despair courage;
that we may be strengthened by the community of saints
to continue our journey of faith;
in Christ's name. Amen

Stuart Burgess

Give thanks
for God's
faithful departed
servants who have
revealed his grace
and enriched our
Christian
pilgrimage

day 30

Renew your whole Church, O Lord, with the spirit of unity and promise, that it may desire only your Kingdom, seek only your will, and be driven only by the mission of its one true and living head; even Jesus Christ our Lord. Amen

Olive Wyon, 1881-1966

 **in Southern Europe**

Portugal

Bishop:
Sifredo Teixeira
rt   Cora Aspey

Lord Jesus, we praise you for all brothers and sisters who have given us support! We ask you now, as they also help other Churches, to continue blessing them, and help us to find ways to be more self-sufficient.

Lord, you know that we are always struggling to face different issues. Help us to be aware of your presence. Give us strength and guidance through your Holy Spirit to find the best way to continue serving you. When bad news seems to dominate, help us to be 'good news' in your name. Amen

Sifredo Teixeira

Spain
Iglesia
Evangelica
Española

President:
Joel Cortès

Give thanks for faithfulness and vision.

Local churches are trying to help asylum seekers who are pouring into Spain from Africa, Eastern Europe and South America. The Church has opened three centres to help refugees and there is deep concern about their integration into the community. Pray with them in this situation.

Pray with the Church's leadership seeking to encourage more lay participation by using part-time ministers.

Italy

Methodist President:
Massimo Aquilante

Give thanks for the strength and ecumenical spirit of this small Church and its vision to become 'a multi-cultural Church where Christian friendship can really be lived and touched'.

Pray for mission to meet changing needs, especially as immigrants continue to pour into the country and congregations grow;

for the work and future of the Casa Materna Home as it struggles with its financial viability and as it explores new ways of working with vulnerable children;

for Pastor George Grant Ennin (NMA), enabling evangelistic work among African immigrant communities in North Italy;

for Vivian Wiwoloku (Director) and Evelyn Aghom (NMA) and Pelligrino del Terra (Pilgrims of the Earth) project in Sicily as it seeks to rescue wome from prostitution and the illicit sex trade.

Give thanks for new District groups such as Taking Care and Lay Training, whose energies and commitment help resource the circuits' witness and mission.

Pray for the work of the National Sponsoring Body for Scotland in encouraging and enabling more flexible ecumenical ventures and partnerships such as the Granton Waterfront project set amid new property development.

Scotland District

Chair:
James Jones

Secretary:
Janet Murray

Give thanks for the renewal of our building at Westerskeld, enabling it to be used in new ways for mission and service.

Pray for the new District Chair Jeremy Dare, his wife Sheila and daughter Marianne, as they begin a new life in Shetland; for all those whose livelihood depends on the declining fishing industry, facing an uncertain future.

Shetland District

Chair:
Jeremy Dare

Secretary:
Sylvia White

For asylum seekers

Lord Jesus, you were tried by a kangaroo court,
humiliated, tortured and killed to be in solidarity with us.
Have mercy on all who suffer the same fate today,
especially those who come here seeking asylum.
Forgive us for the malice of our press,
for the hard-heartedness of our politicians
for the unfair decisions of our adjudicators,
and for the unwelcoming attitude of many of our fellow citizens.
Lord, make your Church in this country a welcoming Church,
and by your stripes may we all be healed. Amen

Jenny Gibson, Sierra Leone/UK

Dear God, thank you for the joy of knowing you, and of being known by you; for your love, your guidance, and your providence in our lives. Help us to live in such a way that our relationship to you is obvious to all. Keep our minds on your scriptures, our hearts open to your Holy Spirit, and help us to see the world through your eyes. Help us never to miss an opportunity to speak of your love through your Son, Jesus, and put in our hearts a desire to hear you say to us one day, 'Well done, good and faithful servant!' Amen

George Freeman, General Secretary, World Methodist Council

Give thanks for our foretaste of the life of the world to come

O God of many names and the lover of all nations, we pray for peace in our hearts, peace in our homes, and peace in our world; the peace of your will and the peace of our need; through Christ our Lord. Amen

George Appleton, 1902-1993

Praying with the whole creation

South to South scholarships:
Esmel Amari° (from Côte d'Ivoire to Cameroon)
Edi Atte° (from Côte d'Ivoire to Cameroon)
Edwin Encinas Ayala° (from Bolivia to Argentina)
Kpoti Lassey° (from Togo to Cameroon)
Charles Loba° (from Côte d'Ivoire to Cameroon)
Marilia Louzada (from Brazil to Spain)
Suirengliana (from Myanmar to S Korea)
Susan Mathiu (from Kenya to S Africa)
Terence Satkunanayagam (Sri Lanka)
Mereia Votomosi (a Fijian within Fiji)
Daw Zothansiami (from Myanmar to India)

Author of creation, we stand in awe of you.
Gazing on the wonders you have made,
we see your glory and receive your blessing
in all that we see, hear, smell, touch and taste.
You have made us creative, in your image,
and so we offer all that we are, every part,
a living sacrifice for you.
With gifts of music, art, drama and dance
we give you our praise and worship.
Make our lives a witness to your glory in creation.

Rachel Appleyard,
Creative Arts and Communications Youth Worker

O God, the kindly encourager,
may your love-light delve down
deeply beneath the
surface of my days
and bring my winter-bound
being to life,
that energised with delight
I might reach upwards and embrace you,
opening out my true self
and offering all that I am to the world you cherish.

Words and image: David W Perry

Loving God, you bless your creation
with beauty and abundance.
Teach us to reverence you in everything you have created,
and help us to be good stewards of all that you entrusted to us,
for the benefit of humankind, and to your praise and glory. Amen

Nicholas Darby, former Rector of Kew, now serving
at the Anglican Cathedral in Gabarone, Botswana

Water – A meditation

Imagine you are an African woman, a single mother with five children ... There is no water supply in your village, and you have nearly two miles to walk to the nearest bore-hole to draw water. You must bring home enough to supply all your family's needs: water for drinking, cooking, for six people to have a wash, to wash all your clothes, clean the house and water your small shamba, a garden where you grow what food you can. You have a few chickens and they can't survive without water either. You have to carry this water in a large metal container on your back. It weighs at least 40 kilos, and is held by a band hooked to your forehead.

On the way to work each day you also collect firewood for cooking and to keep you and the family warm when the night is cold. This too you carry on your back on top of the metal container. You still have a baby and carry her as well ... Life is hard, and the water precious.

Read 2 Samuel 23.13-17 and/or John 4.5-8

Generous God, forgive us that we turn the tap and forget how precious is this gift of water. Forgive our waste. Forgive the little we have done to provide clean water for all.

We pray with those who must continue to walk several miles to draw water ...
for those whose land is dry: who pray for rain and it does not come; whose crops, livestock and children die ...
for communities where the water is contaminated and carries disease ...
for those whose homes and livelihood are destroyed when too much water floods their land ...
for people whose land is threatened by global warming and a rise in sea levels ...

Loving God,
as we rejoice with villages where clean water can now be drawn – through the work of Christian Aid and other development agencies – make us thoughtful when we take water to drink, to enjoy a bath, to cook ...
Strengthen our resolve to care for all that you created, that we may be worthy of the water of life that you have so lavishly given us in Jesus Christ. Amen
Maureen Edwards

Mission Partners and others recently returned from overseas:
Richard Brunt (China)
Heather and Michael Chester (Kenya)
Ros Colwill (Nigeria)
Janet Field (Zambia)
Richard and Carol Grocott (Italy)
Joanne Hall (The Gambia)
Anne Hanks (India)
Kathryn Larrad (Ghana)
Leslie Middleton-Weaver (Sri Lanka)
Alan Moss (China)
Muriel Rogers (Fiji)
Jessica Searle (Uruguay)
Naomi Sharp (Cambodia)
Graham and Sandie Shaw (Zimbabwe)
Jennie Sleep (Nigeria)
Mark Tyers (Grenada)
Dietmar and Birgit Ziegler (RIP Kenya)

Mission Partners in transit or in training:
Colin and Muriel Barrett
Tony Brazier
Janet Corlett
Alison Facey and Chris Esdaile
Rosemary Fletcher and James Rowley
Augusto and Mirna Giron
David and Sarah Hall
Richard and Kathryn Jackson
Jeanna Schofield
Katherine Thomas

Give thanks for the communion of saints

Readings, Hymns and Psalms 2004/5

Readings are broadly based on the International Bible Reading Association's *Words for Today* (2004 & 2005). Psalms are broadly based on the Methodist Sacramental Fellowship's *The Divine Office* (1975). The New Revised Standard Version of the Bible has been used during preparation. Occasionally readings have been changed to respect special occasions recognized by the Methodist Church and various 'holy days'. The contents of this lectionary have been compiled by Philip Turner and Norman Wallwork.

Abbreviations:　　　　HP = Hymns & Psalms (1983)　　　　Ps = Psalm

Week beginning 29 August 2004: 22nd in Ordinary Time
The Glory of Creation

S	29	Hebrews 13:1-16	HP75	Ps 81
M	30	Genesis 1:11-13	HP572	Ps 65
T	31	Genesis 1:20-25	HP332	Ps 2
W	1	Matthew 6:25-33	HP571	Ps 104:10-18
T	2	Job 39:1-8, 26-30	HP338	Ps 5
F	3	Genesis 1:26-31	HP353	Ps 7
S	4	Proverbs 8:22-31	HP336	Ps 9

Week beginning 5 September: 23rd in Ordinary Time
Creation: Spoiled and Restored

S	5	Philemon	HP520	Ps 139
M	6	Deuteronomy 28:15-19, 38-42	HP420	Ps 10
T	7	Isaiah 24:4-13	HP343	Ps 107:33-38
W	8a	Galatians 4:4-7	HP86	Ps 45:10-17
T	9	Deuteronomy 28:1-14	HP430	Ps 23
F	10	Isaiah 32:9-20	HP540	Ps 27
S	11	Isaiah 35:1-7	HP423	Ps 28

[a = The Blessed Virgin Mary]

Week beginning 12 September: 24th in Ordinary Time
Urban Life

S	12b	1 Timothy 1:12-17	HP410	Ps 14
M	13	Genesis 11:1-4	HP412	Ps 49
T	14	Genesis 4:8-17	HP425	Ps 122
W	15	Ezekiel 27:12-24	HP674	Ps 51
T	16	Amos 5:4-17	HP409	Ps 52
F	17	Amos 4:1-6; 6:1, 4-7	HP414	Ps 53
S	18	Acts 14.1-20	HP481	Ps 48:1-14

[b = Racial Justice Sunday]

Week beginning 19 September: 25th in Ordinary Time
Places Jesus Visited

S	19	1 Timothy 2:1-7	HP400	Ps 79
M	20	Matthew 4:1-11	HP235	Ps 55
T	21c	Matthew 9:9-13	HP230	Ps 119:65-72
W	22	Matthew 23:37-38	HP45	Ps 56
T	23	Mark 14:32-42	HP169	Ps 57
F	24	Hebrews 13:12-14	HP819	Ps 61
S	25	Acts 1:4-8	HP326	Ps 62

[c = Matthew, Apostle & Evangelist]

Week beginning 26 September: 26th in Ordinary Time
Two Cities

S	26	1 Timothy 6:6-19	HP464	Ps 91
M	27	Revelation 18:1-20	HP485	Ps 63
T	28	Revelation 18:21-24	HP454	Ps 65
W	29d	Revelation 12:7-12	HP591	Ps 103
T	30	Revelation 21:22-27	HP501	Ps 69:1-13
F	1	Revelation 22:1-6	HP402	Ps 71:1-14
S	2	Revelation 22:12-17	HP79	Ps 71:15-24

[d = Michael & All Angels]

Week beginning 3 October: 27th in Ordinary Time
Ecclesiastes: Observing Life

S	3	2 Timothy 1.1-14	HP740	Ps 137
M	4	Ecclesiastes 1:1-18	HP769	Ps 73:1-13
T	5	Ecclesiastes 2:1-11	HP533	Ps 73:14-28
W	6	Ecclesiastes 2:12-19	HP674	Ps 77
T	7	Ecclesiastes 2:20-26	HP678	Ps 78.1-7
F	8	Ecclesiastes 3:1-8	HP473	Ps 81
S	9	Ecclesiastes 3:9-22	HP665	Ps 82

Week beginning 10 October: 28th in Ordinary Time
Ecclesiastes: Is Anything New?

S	10	2 Timothy 2:8-15	HP465	Ps 66
M	11	Ecclesiastes 4:1-12	HP753	Ps 84
T	12	Ecclesiastes 4:13-16	HP70	Ps 87
W	13	Ecclesiastes 5:1-7	HP759	Ps 88
T	14	Ecclesiastes 5:8-20	HP412	Ps 89:1-15
F	15	Ecclesiastes 6:1-12	HP414	Ps 89:16-37
S	16	Ecclesiastes 7:1-29	HP790	Ps 90

[Week of Prayer for World Peace]

Week beginning 17 October: 29th in Ordinary Time
Ecclesiastes: Towards Meaning

S	17	2 Timothy 3:14 - 4.5	HP479	Ps 119.97-104
M	18e	Luke 10:1-9	HP10	Ps 147
T	19	Ecclesiastes 8:1 - 9:12	HP668	Ps 96
W	20	Ecclesiastes 9:13-18	HP540	Ps 99
T	21	Ecclesiastes 10:1-20	HP374	Ps 101
F	22	Ecclesiastes 11:1-10	HP437	Ps 105:1-15
S	23	Ecclesiastes 12:1-14	HP765	Ps 106:1-9

[One World Week; e = Luke the Evangelist]

Week beginning 24 October: 30th in Ordinary Time
Our Life in God begins

S	24	2 Timothy 4:6-18	HP688	Ps 65
M	25	Genesis 18:9-15; 21:1-7	HP693	Ps 104:1-23
T	26	Isaiah 43:1-7, 15, 18-19a	HP818	Ps 104:24-35
W	27	Isaiah 46:3-4	HP61	Ps 147
T	28f	Ephesians 2.19-22	HP495	Ps 119:89-36
F	29	Romans 8:18-25	HP600	Ps 149
S	30	Galatians 4:19-20	HP65	Ps 150

[f = Simon & Jude, Apostles]

Week beginning 31 October: 31st in Ordinary Time
Life in God is Formed

S	31	Habakkuk 1:1-4; 2.1-4	HP86	Ps 119.137-144
M	1g	Ephesians 1.11-23	HP816	Ps 149
T	2	1 Kings 6	HP688	Ps 145
W	3	1 Kings 7:13-45	HP808	Ps 144
T	4	Jeremiah 18:1-6	HP788	Ps 103
F	5	Exodus 37	HP653	Ps 139:13-18
S	6	Ephesians 2:4-10	HP167	Ps 93

[g = All Saints' Day]

Week beginning 7 November: 32nd in Ordinary Time
The Vision of God

S	7h	Haggai 1:15b – 2:9	HP654	Ps 145
M	8	Isaiah 33:13-22	HP246	Ps 86
T	9	Deuteronomy 3:23-28	HP29	Ps 85
W	10	2 Kings 6:8-23	HP215	Ps 74:1-12
T	11	Matthew 11:2-6	HP744	Ps 74:12-13
F	12	1 John 3:1-3	HP267	Ps 73:1-13
S	13	Acts 2:14-21	HP321	Ps 73:14-28

[h = Methodist Homes Sunday]

Week beginning 14 November: 33rd in Ordinary Time
Our Life in God Expressed

S	14i	Isaiah 65:17-25	HP358	Ps 98
M	15	Amos 3:3-8	HP23	Ps 44
T	16	Matthew 13:31-34	HP336	Ps 19
W	17	Job 39:9-25	HP338	Ps 26
T	18	Ezekiel 40:1-23	HP454	Ps 19
F	19	Song of Songs 4	HP14	Ps 137:1-6
S	20	Isaiah 40:12-31	HP446	Ps 139

[i = Remembrance Sunday]

Week beginning 21 November: Week Before Advent
Songs of Salvation

S	21j	Jeremiah 23.1-6	HP69	Ps 46
M	22	Judges 5	HP66	Ps 13
T	23	1 Chronicles 16:4-36	HP511	Ps 12
W	24	2 Samuel 6:1-15	HP8	Ps 1
T	25	Exodus 15:1-21	HP194	Ps 149
F	26	Ephesians 5:18-20	HP512	Ps 2
S	27	Revelation 15:2-4	HP821	Ps 8

[Prisons Week; j = Christ the King & Youth Sunday]

Week beginning 28 November: 1st of Advent
Signs of Redemption

S	28	Isaiah 2.1-5	HP50	Ps 122
M	29	Genesis 49:8-13	HP409	Ps 96
T	30	Numbers 24:17-19	HP245	Ps 98
W	1l	Deuteronomy 18:15-21	HP75	Ps 9
T	2	Job 19:23-29	HP731	Ps 50
F	3	2 Samuel 7	HP80	Ps 97
S	4	Jeremiah 23:4-7	HP85	Ps 45

[l = World AIDS Day]

Week beginning 5 December: 2nd of Advent
Messianic Hopes

S	5	Isaiah 11.1-10	HP81	Ps 72
M	6	Daniel 7:1-10	HP811	Ps 110
T	7	Isaiah 9:5-6	HP89	Ps 2
W	8	Isaiah 32:1-8	HP783	Ps 94
T	9	Micah 5:1-5	HP113	Ps 48
F	10	Zechariah 9:1-10	HP81	Ps 67
S	11	Malachi 3:1-4	HP84	Ps 76

Week beginning 12 December: 3rd of Advent
Messianic Hopes

S	12	Isaiah 35:1-10	HP239	Ps 146
M	13	Isaiah 42:1-4	HP235	Ps 7
T	14	Isaiah 53:1-6	HP177	Ps 11
W	15	Isaiah 53:7-12	HP176	Ps 24
T	16	Isaiah 61:1-4	HP322	Ps 25
F	17	Mark 1:1-8	HP82	Ps 53
S	18	Mark 1:9-13	HP129	Ps 110

Week beginning 19 December: 4th of Advent
Already and Not Yet

S	19	Isaiah 7.10-16	HP93	Ps 80
M	20	Matthew 8:18-22	HP154	Ps 89:1-15
T	21	Matthew 11:2-19	HP744	Ps 89:16-37
W	22	Mark 8:27-30	HP249	Ps 145
T	23	Matthew 16:21-28	HP124	Ps 75
F	24	John 13:21-30	HP102	Ps 19
S	25n	Isaiah 52:7-10	HP77	Ps 98

[n = Christmas Day]

Week beginning 26 December: 1st of Christmas
Towards Fulfilment

S	26o	Matthew 2:13-23	HP127	Ps 148
M	27p	1 John 1	HP84	Ps 117
T	28q	Jeremiah 31:15-17	HP265	Ps 124
W	29	1 Corinthians 15:20-28	HP257	Ps 2
T	30	Revelation 1:12-19	HP20	Ps 96
F	31	Revelation 5:1-14	HP243	Ps 98
S	1r	Numbers 6.22-27	HP724	Ps 8

[o = Stephen, Deacon & First Martyr;
p = John, Apostle & Evangelist; q = The Holy Innocents;
r = The Naming & Circumcision of Jesus]

Week beginning 2 January 2005: 2nd of Christmas
The Gift of Wisdom

S	2s	John 1.1-18	HP84	Ps 147
M	3	1 Kings 4:29-34	HP674	Ps 34
T	4	Proverbs 1:1-7	HP769	Ps 27
W	5	Proverbs 2:1-15	HP419	Ps 33
T	6t	Isaiah 60:1-6	HP823	Ps 72
F	7	Daniel 2:20-30	HP51	Ps 36
S	8	Acts 6:1-10	HP436	Ps 62

[s = Covenant Sunday; t = The Epiphany]

Week beginning 9 January: 1st in Ordinary Time
Wisdom for Life

S	9	Isaiah 42:1-9	HP278	Ps 29
M	10	Proverbs 3:13-26	HP16	Ps 66
T	11	Proverbs 8:1-21	HP9	Ps 67
W	12	Proverbs 8:22-36	HP75	Ps 87
T	13	Proverbs 9:1-12	HP29	Ps 145:1-7
F	14	Ecclesiastes 7:1-13	HP437	Ps 145:8-21
S	15	Ecclesiastes 9:13 - 10:4	HP436	Ps 116

Week beginning 16 January: 2nd in Ordinary Time
True Wisdom and False

S	16	Isaiah 49:1-7	HP770	Ps 40
M	17	1 Corinthians 2:1-13	HP289	Ps 97
T	18u	Romans 1:18-25	HP769	Ps 18:1-16
W	19	James 3:13-17	HP687	Ps 18:17-31
T	20	Colossians 1:24 - 2:5	HP719ii	Ps 42
F	21	1 Corinthians 1:18-30	HP231	Ps 104:24-35
S	22	Romans 11:33-36	HP463	Ps 65

[u = Octave of Prayer for Christian Unity begins]

Week beginning 23 January: 3rd in Ordinary Time
Baptism, Temptation and Calling

S	23	Matthew 4:12-23	HP460	Ps 27
M	24	Matthew 3:1-17	HP132	Ps 12
T	25v	Acts 9:1-22	HP701	Ps 67
W	26	Matthew 1:1-17	HP85	Ps 13
T	27w	Matthew 4:1-11	HP131	Ps 19
F	28	Matthew 4:18-22	HP141	Ps 33
S	29	Matthew 4:23-25	HP136	103

[v = Conversion of Paul; w = Holocaust Memorial Day]

Week beginning 30 January: 4th in Ordinary Time
Prayer, Fasting and Faith

S	30x	Matthew 5:1-12	HP139	Ps 15
M	31	Matthew 5:13-20	HP422	Ps 105:1-15
T	1	Matthew 5:21-48	HP150	Ps 107:1-15
W	2y	Luke 2:22-40	HP126	Ps 24
T	3	Matthew 6:1-34	HP557	Ps 107:15-31
F	4	Matthew 7:1-20	HP138	Ps 107:31-43
S	5	Matthew 7:21-29	HP137	Ps 142

[x = World Leprosy Day;
y = The Presentation of Christ in the Temple]

Week beginning 6 February: Week Before Lent
Esther

S	6z	Exodus 24.12-18	HP9	Ps 2
M	7	Esther 1:1 - 2:23	HP717	Ps 144
T	8	Esther 3:1 - 5:14	HP713	Ps 146
W	9aa	Joel 2:1-2, 12-17	HP701	Ps 51
T	10	Esther 6:1 - 8:2	HP714	Ps 7
F	11	Esther 8:3 - 9:19	HP716	Ps 143
S	12	Esther 9:20 - 10:3	HP487	Ps 51

[z = Education Sunday; aa = Ash Wednesday]

Week beginning 13 February: 1st in Lent
Who is this?

S	13	Genesis 2:15-17; 3:1-7	HP417	Ps 32
M	14	John 1:19-34	HP84	Ps 25
T	15	John 1:35-51	HP77	Ps 40
W	16	John 2:1-12	HP137	Ps 130
T	17	John 2:13-25	HP176	Ps 131
F	18	John 3:1-21	HP221	Ps 31:1-8
S	19	John 3:22-36	HP699	Ps 31:9-24

Week beginning 20 February: 2nd in Lent
Signs and Teaching

S	20	Genesis 12.1-4a	HP447	Ps 121
M	21	John 4:1-29	HP817	Ps 77
T	22	John 4:30-45	HP238	Ps 30
W	23	John 4:46-54	HP398	Ps 39
T	24	John 5:1-18	HP150	Ps 102:1-12
F	25	John 5:19-29	HP198	Ps 102:13-28
S	26	John 5:30-47	HP129	Ps 139

Week beginning 27 February: 3rd in Lent
Bread and Light

27	Exodus 17.1-7	HP437	Ps 95
28	John 6:1-40	HP730	Ps 15
1	John 6:41-71	HP611	Ps 22:1-21
2	John 7:1-24	HP711	Ps 22:22-31
3	John 7:25-52	HP318	Ps 23
4ab	John 7:53 - 8:20	HP681	Ps 38:1-9
5	John 8:21-59	HP101	Ps 38:10-22

[ab = Women's World Day of Prayer]

Week beginning 6 March: 4th in Lent
Life for the World

6ac	1 Samuel 16.1-13	HP23	Ps 23
7	John 9:1-22	HP423	Ps 140
8	John 9:23-41	HP463	Ps 86
9	John 10:1-21	HP263	Ps 94
10	John 10:22-42	HP750	Ps 104:1-23
11	John 11:1-27	HP655	Ps 104:24-35
12	John 11:28-57	HP173	Ps 6

[ac = Mothering Sunday]

Week beginning 13 March: 5th in Lent – 1st of the Passion
Jesus' Farewell

13	Ezekiel 37:1-14	HP777	Ps 130
14	John 12:1-50	HP228	Ps 88
15	John 13:1-30	HP145	Ps 122
16	John 13:31 - 14:14	HP756	Ps 130
17	John 14:15-31	HP288	Ps 147
18	John 15:1 - 16:33	HP283	Ps 18:1-16
19ad	Matthew 1.18-25	HP152	Ps 89:27-26

[ad = Joseph of Nazareth]

Week beginning 20 March: Holy Week – 2nd of the Passion
Suffering and Death

20ae	Matthew 21.1-11	HP161	Ps 118
21	John 17:1-26	HP719ii	Ps 36
22	John 18:1-18	HP171	Ps 71
23	John 18:19-40	HP169	Ps 70
24af	John 19:1-16	HP618	Ps 116
25ag	John 19:17-30	HP172	Ps 22
26ah	John 19:31-42	HP202	Ps 31

[ae = Palm Sunday; af = Maundy Thursday; ag = Good Friday; ah = Holy Saturday]

Week beginning 27 March: Easter Week
Christ is Risen!

S	27ai	John 20:1-10	HP188	Ps 118
M	28	John 20:11-18	HP195	Ps 114
T	29	2 Kings 4:25-37	HP196	Ps 111
W	30	Luke 15:11-24	HP203	Ps 116
T	31	Romans 10:11-13	HP213	Ps 16
F	1	John 21:1-8	HP211	Ps 117
S	2	John 21:19b-25	HP190	Ps 121

[ai = Easter Day]

Week beginning 3 April: 2nd of Easter
The Women of Easter

S	3	Acts 2:14a, 22-32	HP192	Ps 16
M	4	Exodus 1:15-17	HP205	Ps 122
T	5	1 Peter 3:1-4	HP204	Ps 123
W	6	1 Samuel 25:23-35	HP207	Ps 124
T	7	1 Timothy 5:16	HP208	Ps 125
F	8	Joshua 6:22-25	HP186	Ps 126
S	9	John 4:28-29	HP187	Ps 127

Week beginning 10 April: 3rd of Easter
Living the Easter Message

S	10	Acts 2:14a, 36-41	HP206	Ps 116
M	11	1 Samuel 17:33-50	HP212	Ps 30
T	12	Genesis 24:12-28	HP269	Ps 57
W	13	2 Kings 5:1-15	HP274	Ps 68:1-18
T	14	Jeremiah 1:6-10	HP272	Ps 103
F	15	Daniel 3:13-30	HP255	Ps 113
S	16	1 Timothy 4:11-16	HP256	Ps 128

Week beginning 17 April: 4th of Easter
Believing the Easter Gospel

S	17	Acts 2:42-47	HP260	Ps 23
M	18	1 Corinthians 15:1-11	HP262	Ps 133
T	19	Mark 8:31-34	HP263	Ps 135
W	20	Hebrews 11:4-12	HP275	Ps 136
T	21	Acts 26:1-9, 19-29	HP278	Ps 145:1-7
F	22	Luke 24:36-43	HP188	Ps 145:8-21
S	23	John 20:24-29	HP205	Ps 146

Week beginning 24 April: 5th of Easter
God Remembering

S	24	Acts 7:55-60	HP242	Ps 31
M	25aj	Acts 15.35-41	HP474	Ps 119:9-16
T	26	Genesis 30:22-24	HP298	Ps 112
W	27	Exodus 2:23-25	HP215	Ps 116
T	28	Exodus 3:7-17	HP219	Ps 129
F	29	Leviticus 26:40-45	HP417	Ps 130
S	30	Ezekiel 16:59-63	HP720	Ps 132

[aj = Mark the Evangelist]

Week beginning 1 May: 6th of Easter
Memorials of Christ

S	1ak	Acts 17.22-31	HP234	Ps 66
M	2	Luke 22:14-20	HP614	Ps 147
T	3	1 Corinthians 11:23-32	HP618	Ps 95:1-11
W	4	Isaiah 49:14-16	HP521	Ps 150
T	5al	Acts 1:6-11	HP197	Ps 47
F	6	Luke 24:13-32	HP201	Ps 24
S	7	Mark 14:3-9	HP206	Ps 15

[ak = Philip & James, Apostles; al = Ascension Day]]

Week beginning 8 May:
7th of Easter – Week in Ascensiontide
The Divine Remembrance

S	8	Acts 1:6-14	HP281	Ps 68:1-10
M	9	Galatians 2:9-10	HP439	Ps 105:1-5
T	10	Exodus 20:8	HP514	Ps 21
W	11	Joshua 1:12-18	HP657	Ps 111
T	12	Isaiah 64:1-9	HP405	Ps 110
F	13	Colossians 4:15-18	HP714	Ps 20
S	14am	Acts 1.15-26	HP702	Ps 15

[am = Matthias the Apostle]

Week beginning 15 May: Pentecost
The Fruit of the Spirit: Love

S	15an	Acts 2.1-21	HP307	Ps 104:24-35b
M	16	1 Corinthians 13:1-3	HP320	Ps 100
T	17	1 Corinthians 13:4-7	HP326	Ps 99
W	18	1 Corinthians 13:8-13	HP310	Ps 48
T	19	Luke 6:27-36	HP325	Ps 145:1-7
F	20	2 Corinthians 6:3-7a	HP322	Ps 145:8-21
S	21	Ephesians 5:25-33	HP321	Ps 46

[Christian Aid Week; an = Pentecost]

Week beginning 22 May: Trinity
The Fruit of the Spirit: Joy

S	22ao	Matthew 28.16-20	HP6	Ps 8
M	23	Isaiah 35	HP347	Ps 99
T	24ap	Isaiah 12	HP744	Ps 130
W	25	Luke 10:17-20	HP492	Ps 93
T	26	Luke 24:44-53	HP664	Ps 33
F	27	Colossians 1:9-14	HP574	Ps 115
S	28	Luke 15:3-10	HP691	Ps 149

[ao = Trinity Sunday & Aldersgate Sunday;
ap = Wesley Day]

Week beginning 29 May: 9th in Ordinary Time
The Fruit of the Spirit: Peace and Patience

S	29	Romans 1:16-17; 3:22-31	HP760	Ps 46
M	30	Revelation 12:7-12	HP766	Ps 3
T	31	Ephesians 2:13-18	HP752	Ps 5
W	1	Isaiah 26:1-4	HP732	Ps 10
T	2	1 Thessalonians 5: 12-14	HP725	Ps 28
F	3	Luke 13:6-9	HP795	Ps 41
S	4	Romans 12:14-21	HP800	Ps 49

Week beginning 5 June: 10th in Ordinary Time
Fruits of the Spirit: Kindness and Generosity

S	5	Romans 9:9-26	HP804	Ps 33
M	6	Romans 2:1-11	HP803	Ps 52
T	7	Colossians 3:12-17	HP799	Ps 56
W	8	Romans 12:6-13	HP793	Ps 61
T	9	2 Corinthians 9:6-15	HP631	Ps 63
F	10	1 Timothy 6:17-19	HP802	Ps 69:1-13
S	11aq	Acts 11:19-30	HP798	Ps 112

[aq = Barnabas the Apostle]

Week beginning 12 June: 11th in Ordinary Time
The Fruit of the Spirit: Faithfulness

S	12	Romans 5.1-8	HP695	Ps 116
M	13	Ruth 2:8-12	HP690	Ps 71:1-14
T	14	Luke 12:42-48	HP708	Ps 71:15-24
W	15	Psalm 119:30-37	HP704	Ps 136
T	16	Titus 2:9-14	HP705	Ps 137
F	17	Philippians 1:27-29	HP711	Ps 138
S	18	Revelation 2:8-11	HP709	Ps 139

[World Refugee Week]

Week beginning 19 June: 12th in Ordinary Time
The Fruit of the Spirit: Gentleness and Self-control

S	19	Romans 6.1-11	HP694	Ps 86
M	20	Ephesians 4:1-6	HP687	Ps 8
T	21	1 Peter 3:13-16	HP688	Ps 12
W	22	Titus 3:2-7	HP692	Ps 15
T	23	Philippians 4:4-7	HP696	Ps 20
F	24ar	Luke 1.57-66, 80	HP264	Ps 85
S	25	Titus 2:1-8	HP697	Ps 24

[ar = John the Baptist]

Translation of prayer on p23

Lord our God, who came amongst us in Jesus Christ,
thank you for the new opportunities which you give to your people;
new relationships with you and with each other.
Use each of us to build bridges with people
and to love and accept others, in the name of Jesus Christ, Amen

Week beginning 26 June: 13th in Ordinary Time
Healing

S	26as	Romans 6.12-23	HP707 Ps 13
M	27	Matthew 8:1-13	HP645 Ps 25
T	28	Matthew 8:14 - 9:1	HP142 Ps 26
W	29at	Acts 12:1-11	HP257 Ps 125
T	30	Matthew 9:2-8	HP735 Ps 42
F	1	Matthew 9:9-17	HP148 Ps 43
S	2	Matthew 9:18 - 10:4	HP390 Ps 46

[as = Methodist Conference Sunday; at = Peter the Apostle]

Week beginning 3 July: 14th in Ordinary Time
Instruction to the Twelve

S	3au	Romans 7:15-25a	HP205 Ps 145
M	4	Matthew 10:5-15	HP139 Ps 47
T	5	Matthew 10:16-23	HP140 Ps 48
W	6	Matthew 10:24-35	HP562 Ps 54
T	7	Matthew 10:34-42	HP431 Ps 68:1-18
F	8	Matthew 12:1-8	HP576 Ps 72
S	9	Matthew 13:1-17	HP540 Ps 74

[au = Thomas the Apostle]

Week beginning 10 July: 15th in Ordinary Time
Lamentations

S	10av	Romans 8:1-11	HP661 Ps 119:105-112
M	11	Lamentations 1.12-22	HP166 Ps 75
T	12	Lamentations 3:1-20	HP228 Ps 76
W	13	Lamentations 3:21-51	HP66 Ps 80
T	14	Lamentations 3:52-66	HP173 Ps 137
F	15	Lamentations 4	HP174 Ps 142
S	16	Lamentations 5	HP713 Ps 143

[av = NCH Sunday]

Week beginning 17 July: 16th in Ordinary Time
Celebrating the Festival

S	17	Romans 8.12-25	HP310 Ps 139
M	18	Exodus 23:14-17	HP353 Ps 110
T	19	2 Chronicles 30:1-21	HP349 Ps 121
W	20	Nehemiah 12:27-43	HP348 Ps 125
T	21	Genesis 21:1-8	HP442 Ps 126:1-6
F	22aw	Luke 8.1-3	HP171 Ps 30
S	23	Revelation 19:6-10	HP278 Ps 131

[aw = Mary Magdalene]

Week beginning 24 July: 17th in Ordinary Time
Peculiar Parties

S	24	Romans 8.26-39	HP823 Ps 105:1-11
M	25ax	Acts 11:27 ñ 12:2	HP141 Ps 126
T	26	Mark 6:21-25	HP761 Ps 133
W	27	Luke 14:1-14	HP460 Ps 135
T	28	Numbers 28:16-26	HP300 Ps 118
F	29	Exodus 32:1-6	HP595 Ps 119:1-16
S	30	Luke 17:26-29	HP290 Ps 119:17-32

[ax = James the Apostle]

Week beginning 31 July: 18th in Ordinary Time
Dancing in Celebration

S	31	Romans 9.1-5	HP254 Ps 17
M	1	2 Samuel 6:1-14	HP563 Ps 150
T	2	Jeremiah 31:1-14	HP491 Ps 119:33-64
W	3	1 Chronicles 15: 25 - 16:3	HP503 Ps 119:65-80
T	4	Acts 3:1-10	HP461 Ps 119:81-96
F	5	Exodus 15:19-21	HP453 Ps 119:97-128
S	6ay	2 Peter 1.16-19	HP156 Ps 97

[ay = The Transfiguration]

Week beginning 7 August: 19th in Ordinary Time
Parables of the Kingdom

S	7	Romans 10:5-15	HP677 Ps 105:16-22
M	8	Matthew 13:24-32	HP474 Ps 119:129-144
T	9	Matthew 13:33	HP218 Ps 119:145-160
W	10	Matthew 13:44-45	HP45 Ps 119:161-176
T	11	Matthew 13:47-50	HP355 Ps 136
F	12	Matthew 13:51-53	HP571 Ps 138
S	13	Matthew 13:54-58	HP383 Ps 140

Week beginning 14 August: 20th in Ordinary Time
Signs and Wonders

S	14	Romans 11.1-2a, 29-32	HP378 Ps 133
M	15	Matthew 14:13-33	HP144 Ps 1
T	16	Matthew 14:34-36	HP148 Ps 2
W	17	Matthew 15:21-28	HP608 Ps 3
T	18	Matthew 15:29-39	HP147 Ps 5
F	19	Matthew 20:28-34	HP423 Ps 7
S	20	Matthew 21:14-22	HP685 Ps 9

Week beginning 21 August: 21st in Ordinary Time
Messages from James & Jude

S	21	Romans 12:1-8	HP801 Ps 124
M	22	James 1:1-18	HP715 Ps 10
T	23	James 2:1-4	HP804 Ps 11
W	24	James 2:14-17	HP405 Ps 16
T	25	James 4:11-12	HP553 Ps 23
F	26	James 5:13-18	HP394 Ps 27
S	27	Jude 3-6	HP487 Ps 28

Week beginning 28 August: 22nd in Ordinary Time
Messages from Peter

S	28	Romans 12:9-21	HP45 Ps 105:23-26
M	29	1 Peter 1:3 - 2:10	HP725 Ps 30
T	30	1 Peter 3:18-22	HP235 Ps 31:1-8
W	31	1 Peter 5:8-11	HP877 Ps 31:9-24
T	1	2 Peter 1:16-18	HP155 Ps 32
F	2	2 Peter 3:8-10	HP245 Ps 34
S	3	2 Peter 3:14-16	HP488 Ps 36

Key

The letters beside the names indicate the type of work in which mission partners are mainly engaged:

ad administration
d doctor
ed education
m medical work
   (other than doctor
   or nurse)
n nursing
p pastoral worker
rt retired
sd social/development
   work
sp special partner
t technical
th theological training
° minister
* deacon

+ **Joint
  Appointment**
USPG United Society
   for the Propagation of
   the Gospel (Anglican)
CMS Church Mission
   Society (Anglican)
CofS Church of
   Scotland
CA Christians Abroad

OMF Overseas
   Missionary
   Fellowship
NMA Nationals in
   Mission Appointments
UCA United College
   of the Ascension
WCBP World Church in
   Britain Partnership

For further information

Called to Prayer – a companion to the Prayer Handbook which includes a selection of prayers from past years and arranges them under the themes of 'Our Calling'.
Price: £9.75 from mph (Methodist Publishing House).

The Methodist Website – www.methodist.org.uk – *includes prayers from the Prayer Handbook and other prayers*

Flame – The Methodist Magazine – a bi-monthly magazine celebrating what it means to be Christian in the Methodist tradition. Subscribe today. *Contact mph.*

Magnet – the magazine of the Women's Network – *available from your local church or circuit distributor. Details of individual subscriptions from the Women's Network Office, Methodist Church House (MCH), 25 Marylebone Road, London NW1 5JR Tel: 020 7486 5502.*

Mission Matters – part of the Link Mailing – *available from mph, four times a year.*

Words for Today (IBRA) – reflections on daily Bible readings from many parts of the world and well-known writers.
Light for our Path (IBRA) – notes for those who need a simpler and less provocative approach. *Both are available from mph.*

The Methodist Recorder – *from your newsagent or from 122 Golden Lane, London EC1Y 0TL.*

Copies of this Prayer Handbook, and a large-print edition (at the same price) – *available from the Methodist Bookshop (at MCH) and mph.*

The Prayer Handbook on Tape – *from the Blind Welfare Society – enquiries in the first instance to the Mission Education Office, MCH.*

Prayer Focus – The Prayer Handbook of the Methodist Church in Ireland – *available from the Methodist Church in Ireland, Aldersgate House, University Road, Belfast BT7 1NA Tel: 028 90 320078.*

Copyright – The prayers in this book are © 2004 Trustees for Methodist Church Purposes, unless otherwise indicated. For permissions, please contact mph.

Printed by **Stanley L Hunt (Printers) Ltd**, Midland Road Rushden, Northamptonshire NN10 9UA.